KAFFE FASSETT'S
country garden quilts

featuring Roberta Horton • Mary Mashuta • Liza Prior Lucy • Pauline Smith • Brandon Mably • Jane Brocket • Sally Davis • Betsy Rickles

A ROWAN BOOK

The Taunton Press

The Taunton Press
Inspiration for hands-on living®

The Taunton Press
63 South Main St PO Box 5506
Newton, CT 06470-5506
www.taunton.com

First Published in Great Britain in 2008 by Rowan Yarns

Art Director: Kaffe Fassett
Technical editors: Ruth Eglinton and Pauline Smith
Co-ordinator: Pauline Smith
Publishing Consultant: Susan Berry
Patchwork Designs: Kaffe Fassett, Roberta Horton,
                       Mary Mashuta, Liza Prior Lucy,
                       Betsy Rickles, Pauline Smith, Sally Davis,
                       Jane Brocket, Brandon Mably.
Feature: Jane Brocket

Quilters: Judy Irish, Pauline Smith
Sewers for Liza Prior Lucy quilts: Judy Baldwin,
                                    Corienne Kramer

Photography: Debbie Patterson
Flat shot photography: Dave Tolson @ Visage

Styling: Kaffe Fassett
Design Layout: Christine Wood - Gallery of Quilts/
                                       cover/front section
                       Simon Wagstaff - instructions &
                                        technical information

Illustrations: Ruth Eglinton

Library of Congress Cataloging-in-Publication Data

Fassett, Kaffee
Kaffe Fassett's country garden quilts: 20 designs from Rowan for
patchwork and quilting / Kaffee Fassett.
p. cm. -- (Patchwork and quilting book: no.10)
"A Rowan book."
Includes bibliographical references and index.
ISBN 978-1-60085-048-6
1. Patchwork--Patterns. 2 Quilting--Patterns. I. Rowan Yarns.
II. Title. III. Title: Country garden quilts.

TT835.F3673 2008
746.46'041--dc22
2008018959

Colour reproduction by Chroma Graphics (Overseas) Pte. Ltd
Printed and bound in Singapore

contents

introduction

It was a great honour for me to be able to photograph our newest quilt collection in the famous Great Dixter garden in East Sussex, developed by Christopher Lloyd, who was one of the most innovative of gardeners in Great Britain and an influential author of many gardening books and articles. Like me, he was in love with the power of colour and seemed never to tire of trying new combinations and encouraging other gardeners to be more experimental.

As Christopher said, "Rules, it has to be said, are made to be broken" and "Go for it would be my motto". So, as we placed our quilts in front of or actually in the luscious borders of Dixter, I couldn't help feeling that these colourful beds were living patchworks. Here, as if to prove the point, is another quote from Christopher: "I have a constant awareness of colour and of what I am doing, but if I think a yellow candelabrum of mullein will look good rising from the middle of a quilt of pink phlox, I'll put it there."

We photographed most of the quilts on a glorious autumn day but had to return to finish the job in early spring. After seeing the garden in its high end of summer colour it was then interesting to see the beginning stages with bulbs and plants starting to break through the rich earth. When our shots came back I was delighted to see how Christopher Lloyd's colours and the architecture of the house set off our quilts. Built in the middle of the 15th century, the house was restored and enlarged by Sir Edwin Lutyens in 1910 – the restoration revealed the medieval splendour of the Great Hall, the largest surviving timber-framed hall in England.

All of us doing patchworks for this book responded to the possibility of the exciting floral displays we knew we would find in a Christopher Lloyd garden by heightening our colours and using lots of new florals. We hope you enjoy the results.

As far as my quilts are concerned, you will see I have done my usual thing of making two versions of some of them. That is to encourage you all to use your own personal colour preferences in any of the "recipes" for quilts you find here. The *S Block Quilt* was a delicious graphic layout that is easy

OPPOSITE: *Double Pinwheels Quilt*
BELOW: *Blue Economy Patch Quilt*

to sew and could be done in millions of versions. I went for a sunny yellow floral that looks so good against a golden tree at Dixter and a more abstract stripe version, *Earthy S Block Quilt* in shot cotton and the close-toned new woven stripes from India which are perfect for this sort of project. It was set off superbly by the moss-covered barns. The other quilt I've done in two versions is *Floral Star Bouquet*: first a spring-like floral version that graces our cover and then a deep passionate red one that should warm the winter nights or brighten up a sitting room if draped over a sofa.

I was delighted to invite Jane Brocket, a young English quilter who has a simple approach to design and a passion for English gardens and allotments, to do a version of her *Allotment Quilt* specially for this book. In Patchwork Gardening (see page 52) you can see this first *Allotment Quilt* and read about her design ideas.

BELOW LEFT: *Yellow S Block Quilt*
BELOW RIGHT: *Earthy S Block Quilt*

RIGHT: *Red Star Bouquet Quilt*
BELOW RIGHT: *Pastel Star Bouquet Quilt*

the fabrics

Floral Brocade

Loving brocades I decided to do my own. To dress it up with a bit of extra colour, I placed a bouquet of jaunty flowers every repeat of the print. I'm glad to report that it's a very useful addition to many quilts. You can fussy cut the flowers for a floral element or just cut the brocade, or use as a brocade with a surprise element. I like the way it looks in my *Pastel Star Bouquet*.

Bekah

One of the best quiltmakers I know lives in Houston, Texas, has brilliant red hair and loves roses in her quilts. When I dreamed up my large floral in the original colourway of oranges, reds, and yellows we all said 'Bekah will love this one, lets name it after her.'

Spot and Aboriginal Dots

Polka dots have always delighted me but I felt so many people do them that there would be no call for my versions on the old theme, how wrong I was. When we released the first polka dots in our particular colours they were an instant hit and have proved wildly useful to us in our quilt designs. Aboriginal Dots was a subtle variation that makes a brocade like ground that is almost solid and equally useful.

Jungle Stripe

Classic old woven and embroidered Paisleys have always moved me with their elegant dancing forms. When they are organised into stripes I like it even more, so I did my version of Paisley stripes. It makes lively borders and is an exciting stripe to make stars and boxes in your patchwork. I was intrigued to see how Jungle Stripe would look with Targets cut into large equilateral triangles so we made up a sample piece (see bottom left). Although it isn't a finished quilt and there are no instructions we decided to show it as an idea which you could easily make up. A wide strip of Jungle Stripe would make a handsome border.

Targets

I did a mosaic wall for the Highland Stoneware Potteries in Scotland. They made me tiles and plates of contrasting circular stripes that were very exciting to break up and reassemble as mosaic. All the time I was mosaicking I kept thinking that patchworkers would love using cut up circles so I designed Targets the moment I got home. It appears in many of the quilts in the book, often as a border.

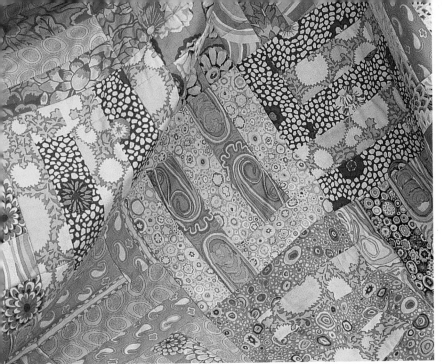

Pinking Flower

Antique Suzani embroideries have inspired me for years. It is a great joy to finally get down to use that inspiration in Pinking Flower. The middle eastern embroideries often had those lovely jagged edges on their dark red circular flowers that remind me of fabric cut with pinking shears.

The Latest Fabrics

Many of the quilts were already done when we received the newest fabric from the printers, but a couple of quilts include some of these new fabrics. A new version of Pressed Rose we now call Silhouette Rose is in new fresh colours. I used the duck egg colourway to frame the centre panel in *Chintz* quilt.

My favourite design is Lichen inspired by the wondrous lichens found in Britain. It's a new exciting twist on a floral which I've used in my *Red Star Bouquet* quilt.

Philip Jacobs has just come out with gorgeous big florals that I've added my colours to. I've used them in *Chintz* quilt where they mix well with some of the old favourite florals from the collection.

We have for the first time included a collection of Arts and Crafts prints. You can see some of these in *Red Star Bouquet* quilt. We have convinced Rowan to develop a classic range so you can revisit some of your favourites and use them alongside the new collections. You will notice how we've used Lotus Leaf, Zinnia, Roman Glass, Paper weight , Cloisonne, Paperfans, Kimono, Flower Basket, Jungle Paisley and Dahlia Blooms, and love mixing them with the new ones. As I colour up new designs I refer to the classic colours to make sure they all work together."

Zig Zag by Liza Prior Lucy
Liza's stunning quilt is cleverly pieced from my Jungle Stripe fabric, which is
fussy cut to make the most of the stripes and Spot in hot reds and magenta.

Garden Whirligig by Mary Mashuta
Mary has grown her own joyful flower
garden.Bekah, one of my favourite large florals is a
great choice for the border.

Bekah's Basket Sampler by Betsy Rickles
There is a degree of formality about Betsy's quilt
which pleases me. The low ivy clad barn roof and
golden chrysanthemums look just right.

Diagonal Madness by Kaffe Fassett
The 9 - patch border makes a great frame for this quilt.
The rich colours in the quilt are echoed by the salvias,
petunias and rudbeckia in the flowerpots. The detail
shows the 4-patch columns.

Pastel Star Bouquet by Kaffe Fassett
A glimpse of the manor house is the backdrop for the
pastel version of *Star Bouquet*. The detail shows the
exciting way the sashing frames the large floral block
centres, making stars at the corners.

Yellow S Block by Kaffe Fassett
My quilt glimpsed through the columns of yew. I took
the yellow and gold prints from my latest fabrics and
old favourites for this quilt made from a simple block.

The Gift by Brandon Mably
Brandon's charming baby quilt has a bold bow in dramatic reds appliqued over high pastels. The detail shows the stitching on the bow.

Blooms by Pauline Smith
The tropical planting makes an exotic backdrop for Pauline's quilt. My blue Aboriginal Dot cools down the hot blooms.

Double Pinwheel by Liza Prior Lucy
The intense colours of Liza's quilt are in harmony with the bed of gold chrysanthemums. The quilt looks good displayed against the backdrop of the manor house at Great Dixter designed by Edwin Lutyens. The large floral pinwheels are bordered by tiny pinwheels in jewel-like colours.

Economy Blue Patch by Liza Prior Lucy
As soon as I stepped into this enclosed garden with its lavender and
pink flowers I knew it would be perfect to show off Liza's quilt which
uses just about every blue fabric in the range.

Garden Rainbow by Roberta Horton
The considered choice of fabric in just the right shade makes Roberta's
quilt truly a rainbow. The lily pond sets it off a treat.

Knot Garden by Kaffe Fassett
The cool pastel palette of blue, lavender and lime sits well against the terracotta pots in front of the shed.

Right on Target by Sally Davis
Sally's fun quilt, hanging in the timbered barn, showcases my pastel Target fabric. The detail shows the alternating log cabin blocks.

Spider Web by Kaffe Fassett
The topiary columns of Great Dixter add drama to my
Spider Web. I am thrilled with how the red Targets
border adds the finishing touch to my quilt.

Windmills by Pauline Smith
Pauline had hot dahlias and windmill bird scarers in mind when she designed this quilt, so this is the perfect spot to show it off.

Chintz by Kaffe Fassett
I saw a wonderful quilt in an Australian book on vintage quilts. It was made of classic English chintz fabrics and I just couldn't resist trying to create it in my fabrics. The soft colours glow against the silvered half timbered framing of Great Dixter. Philip Jacob's Lilac Rose makes an elegant centre panel for the *Chintz Quilt.*

Paisley Stars by Kaffe Fassett
My jungle stripe fabric comes totally into its own in this bold star quilt, you might say it was made for the purpose. The border is one of my all time favourites. Borrowed from an old English quilt it has a dramatic sense of dimension.

Red Star Bouquet by Kaffe Fassett
How richly dramatic the *Red Star Bouquet Quilt* looks on the fabulous topiary birds at Great Dixter. You can see what a great showcase for upscale prints the quilt is with its large framed squares.

Earthy S Block by Kaffe Fassett
Making this block with my woven Indian Stripes gives it a powerfully graphic appearance. How different the mood from the *Yellow S Block* with its voluptuous florals. I'm always moved by the vivid moss colour on some English barns and fences in the winter.

Allotment by Jane Brocket
The simple structure of Jane's quilt allows her to explore many possible combos of Philip's and my floral prints in colours suggested by an English allotment in late summer.

patchwork gardening

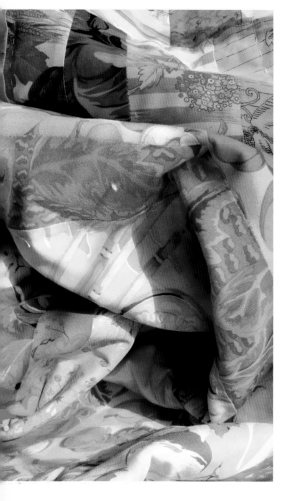

When I was fourteen, I was banned from the art room at school and told to study academic subjects. I think the rest of my life, creatively speaking, has been a rebellion against this short-sighted decision.

As a result, I've always been something of an enthusiastic, if untrained, dabbler in crafts. As a teenager I made up for the lack of creativity and colour and experimentation at school by using my bedroom as a studio for tie-dyeing, candle-making, leather-belt production, macramé, growing herbs and spraying gold pasta collages. I spent my money on squares of felt, sequins, ribbons, beads, fabrics, and sparkly stuff and was always happiest with glue and scissors and needles and threads.

I learned to sew when I was eleven on my Nana's old Singer sewing-machine which had been converted to run on electricity. In my teens I made a few clothes and soft toys and loved scouring markets and shops for fabrics. Although I put the machine away when I went to university and took up knitting instead, I continued to wander wistfully round fabric stores trying to imagine what I could make.

So, with my love of fabric, pattern, colour and design, it was inevitable that one day I would decide I wanted to quilt. But, even then, I still found myself stuck due to my lack of artistic training or background; apart from a few workshops here and there, I am completely self-taught when it comes to making things. Although this has never posed too much of a problem when it comes to knitting, crochet, embroidery, beading and so on (in fact, it has been incredibly liberating in many ways), I thought it *was* a problem with quilting. I was convinced that there were right and wrong ways to make a quilt, that I didn't have sufficient skills and know-how, and that I wasn't 'qualified' to make one.

That is, until the late 1990s when I discovered that my knitting guru, Kaffe Fassett, was shaking up the world of patchwork with his messages of fun, colour, experimentation and most importantly, his refrain of 'just have a go' in beautiful, technicolour, exuberant books written with the gifted and talented Liza Prior Lucy. Even then, I have to confess that it was years after buying *Glorious Patchwork* that I took my first, hesitant steps in quilting.

And then, goodness me, it would seem that 'having a go' unleashed a lifetime of subconscious quilt designs which were waiting to be made. My first attempt was a simple, vivid, silk square quilt, and I haven't looked back since. We now have quilts all over the house - on beds, chairs, settees — and I find there is nothing more rewarding than seeing someone snuggled up in a quilt I have made. These days, I have at least one quilt (sometimes two) in production at all times, and at least another two or three either sitting either in my imagination or in piles of fabrics

I'm not terribly ambitious and I have come to realise that, rather than working on complex designs, I really enjoy using simple shapes such as strips, squares and rectangles which work as vehicles for fabulous fabrics. This is partly to do with the fact that my skills don't stretch to triangles and curves and diamonds (yet – I may try one day) and also because I still feel I am working my way through all the wonderful colour schemes and patterns which have been floating around in my mind for years and which I want to create relatively quickly and painlessly after all those years of suppression.

And even though I have broadened my horizons and value many different sources of inspiration such as Denyse Schmidt, Roberta Horton, the quilts of Gee's Bend, the quilts in The American Museum in Bath and in beautiful Japanese books, Kaffe and Liza continue to be my greatest inspirations. So it is fitting that it was when I travelled to Stockholm for a weekend in October 2006 to see Kaffe's exhibition at the Waldemarsudde that I first thought of making an allotment quilt.

After seeing the wonderful quilts and knitting in the perfect setting of a furnished house (it was bequeathed to the nation in 1947 by Prince Eugen, himself an artist of note) I wandered around the extensive organic, allotment-style gardens belonging to the Rosendals Tradgard. I was bowled over by the rich autumnal yellows and golds of the trees, the sunflowers and the nasturtiums, the deep greens of the spinach and cabbages, and the brilliant pinks of the cosmos, ruby chard and zinnias. I wanted to capture this startlingly beautiful scene in a quilt, and realised that the row by row, allotment approach would be perfect.

I like the way that allotment holders here in the UK take a bare patch of land which usually measures ten rods (allotments are measured in quaint, archaic language; ten rods equals approximately 3000 square feet, usually 30 feet wide and 100 feet long) and then fill their rectangles with strips and rows and blocks and borders full of flowers and vegetables and

fruit. In the same way, the quilter can take a basic shape and fill it with beautiful fabrics and patterns.

So I made a basic rectangular layout of two columns, each the full width of my fabrics, then filled it in with various lengths of flowers, seeds, vegetables and fruits which I pre-cut in random lengths. I 'grew' it by building it up strip by strip, shortening or lengthening sections where necessary, preferring each strip to look good next to its neighbour but not insisting that it co-ordinated perfectly and tastefully with other parts. The aim was for each strip to be absorbed into the whole and yet still stand out and catch the eye, and I discovered that if I tried to over-plan and use repeats or patterns, my quilt started to lack the impression of spontaneity and joie de vivre.

Then, just as there are paths and borders through and around allotments, I added a double border to hold the diversity of produce together (my fabrics feature vegetables, seeds, flowers and fruit). When I came to the backing fabric, I found I didn't have enough of my chosen fabric, so added a thick strip of a Martha Negley vegetable design next to the main Wisteria fabric in Tobacco.

I wanted my quilt to embody the allotment culture which so fascinates and reassures me. I like the mix – both visually and philosophically - of improvisation, recycling and pragmatism which is evident in the way allotments are laid out, cultivated and maintained. It reflects my own ideas about the way I prefer to make quilts – they don't have to be perfect, they incorporate scraps and leftovers, and I enjoy improvising backs and borders and bindings. I would much rather have a quilt finished and ready to brighten a room and keep a body warm, than worry about what people might say if my hand-quilting goes a little wobbly or my corners don't turn out with precision mitres.

The second *Allotment Quilt* was made in summer and is more 'High Summer in England' in feel. I was inspired by the sheer fertility of English allotments and their profusion of produce and wanted to include some rich, earthy browns to suggest the cared-for and well-manured soil. And then I chose a rich mixture of scarlet for runner bean flowers, deep reds for dahlias, purples for beetroot, lime greens for lettuces, lemon yellows for sunflowers and oranges for gladioli. There are strips of polka dots for seeds and seedlings, and the back is a wickedly, mouth-watering zonal geranium print reflect the bright, cheerful geraniums which sit in ramshackle potting sheds and along the edges of plots.

Since my first quilt, I've enjoyed thinking of all different allotments I'd like to design according to seasons. A spring quilt could be all pinks, fresh greens, pale blues and blossom colours, a summer version would be made up of brights such as cerise, orange, purple, the azure of clear blue skies, the scarlets of strawberries and the emerald greens of healthy leaves. An autumnal quilt would feature burnished bronzes, golds, garnets, deep hedge, privet, and french bean greens, the rich deep jewel colours of dahlias and berries, while a winter theme would mirror the allotments when they are bare and stripped and would be a delicate but graphic mix of greys, golds, browns, pale blues and silvers, frosts, nut browns and dried seed-head blacks.

The allotment quilt is a vehicle for individual taste and expression, so I think it would be marvellous to see a collection made by different people and brought together like one enormous, colourful, flamboyant landscape. Within the one, single framework there would be such a brilliant diversity of colours, designs, personalities – just as there is when you visit a real allotment site – and a fabulous juxtaposition of the neat and orderly and tidy, next to the relaxed, informal, shaggy. There would be variations in scale, levels of perfection and fabrics, and yet every single one would be grown and sewn with enthusiasm and enjoyment. For the therapy of indoor allotment quilt making is not far removed from that of outdoor allotments; both rectangles offer huge opportunities for experimentation.

Just as each year is a chance to start again with fresh, blank rectangle of fertile earth, each quilt provides a chance to make a more permanent allotment. And the great thing is that you don't have to wait until spring to start.

Jane Brocket
November 2007

Pastel Star Bouquet Quilt ★★★

KAFFE FASSETT

Although this quilt features large simple squares of print the pieced star sashing gives it a dynamic excitement that keeps the eye wandering. I'm always happy when I find a new way to use my big florals in a generous expanse.

SIZE OF QUILT
The finished quilt will measure approx.
75in x 75in (190.5cm x 190.5cm).

MATERIALS
Patchwork Fabrics:
DAHLIA BLOOMS
Succulent	GP54SC: ⅜yd (35cm)
Vintage	GP54VN: ⅜yd (35cm)

GUINEA FLOWER
Mauve	GP59MV: ¾yd (70cm)
Pink	GP59PK: ⅜yd (35cm)

PINKING FLOWER
Pink	GP66PK: ¾yd (70cm)
Red	GP66RD: ¼yd (25cm)

BROCADE FLORAL
Lavender	GP68LV: ½yd (45cm)*
Pink	GP68PK: 1yd (90cm)*

BEKAH
Blue	GP69BL: ⅜yd (35cm)
Orange	GP69OR: ⅝yd (60cm)
Pastel	GP69PT: ⅝yd (60cm)

SPOT
Duck Egg	GP70DE: ¼yd (25cm)

Fuchsia	GP70FU: ⅜yd (35cm)
Magenta	GP70MG: ¾yd (70cm)
Mint	GP70MT: ½yd (45cm)
Red	GP70RD: ⅜yd (35cm)
Turquoise	GP70TQ: ⅜yd (35cm)

ABORIGINAL DOTS
Blue	GP71BL: ¼yd (25cm)
Rose	GP71RO: ⅜yd (35cm)

SHOT COTTON
Brick	SC58: ¼yd (25cm)

SINGLE IKAT WASH
Red	SIW06: ⅜yd (35cm)

*Extra fabric allowed for fussy cutting.

Backing Fabric: 5⅜yds (4.9m)
We suggest these fabrics for backing:
DAHLIA BLOOMS Succulent, GP54SC
PINKING FLOWER Pink, GP66PK
BROCADE FLORAL Pink, GP68PK

Binding:
SPOT
Fuchsia   GP70FU: ¾yd (70cm)

Batting:
83in × 83in (211cm × 211cm).

Quilting thread:
Pink machine quilting thread.

Templates:

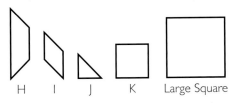

H   I   J   K   Large Square

PATCH SHAPES
The main block which finishes to 13in (33cm) uses 3 patch shapes, 1 large square (cut to size) 1 diamond patch shape (Template I) and a lozenge patch shape (Template H). The blocks are straight set into rows and where the blocks intersect a pretty star pattern is seen. The centre section is surrounded with a border pieced from 'Square in a Square' blocks which finish to 5in (12.75cm). These blocks are made using 1 square (Template K) and 1 triangle patch shape (Template J). The border has corner posts which are cut to size.

CUTTING OUT
Cut the fabric in the order stated to prevent waste.
Large Square: Cut 9½in (24.25cm) strips across the width of the fabric. Each strip will give you 4 patches per width. Cut 9½in (24.25cm) squares, cut 6 in GP69OR, 4 in GP69PT, 3 in GP54SC, GP54VN, GP68LV*, GP68PK* and GP69BL.
* Note: These fabrics were fussy cut to centre large blooms.
Border Corner Posts: Fussy cut 4 × 5½in (14cm) squares in GP68PK centring on large blooms.
Template H: Cut 2½in (6.25cm) strips across the width of the fabric. Each strip will give you 6 patches per width. Cut 27 in GP66PK, 22 in SIW06, 15 in GP71RO, 13 in GP68PK, 12 in SC58 and 11 in GP59MV.
Template I: Cut 2½in (6.25cm) strips across the width of the fabric. Each strip will give you 10 patches per width. Cut 29 in GP70FU, GP70TQ, 27 in GP59PK, 24 in GP70RD, 20 in GP66RD, 18 in GP70DE,

GP70MT, GP71BL and 17 in GP68LV.
Template J: Cut 3⅜in (8.5cm) strips across the width of the fabric. Each strip will give you 22 patches per width. Cut 104 in GP59MV and GP70MG.
Template K: Cut 4in (10.25cm) strips across the width of the fabric. Each strip will give you 10 patches per width. Cut 15 in GP66PK, 14 in GP69PT, 12 in GP70MT, 10 in GP68PK and 1 in GP69BL.

Binding: Cut 8 strips 2½in (6.5cm) wide across the width of the fabric in GP70FU.

Backing: Cut 2 pieces 40in × 83in (101.5cm × 211cm), 2 pieces 40in × 4in (101.5cm × 10.25cm) and 1 piece 4in × 4in (10.25cm × 10.25cm) in backing fabric. Note: For a quirky look to the backing you could cut the 4in square from a different fabric and piece the backing with the contrasting square in the centre.

MAKING THE MAIN BLOCKS
Use a ¼in (6mm) seam allowance throughout. Refer to the quilt assembly diagram for fabric placement. For the main blocks the inset seam method is used (see Patchwork Knowhow on page 137). Inset seams are fiddly to do, but get much easier with a little practice, we have found it is better to stitch all the blocks to this stage and then complete all the inset seaming

Block Assembly Diagrams

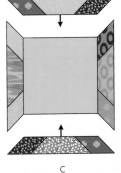

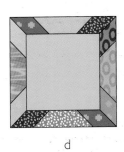

a   b   c   d

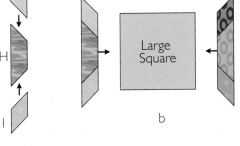

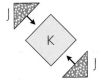

e   f   g

Quilt Assembly Diagram

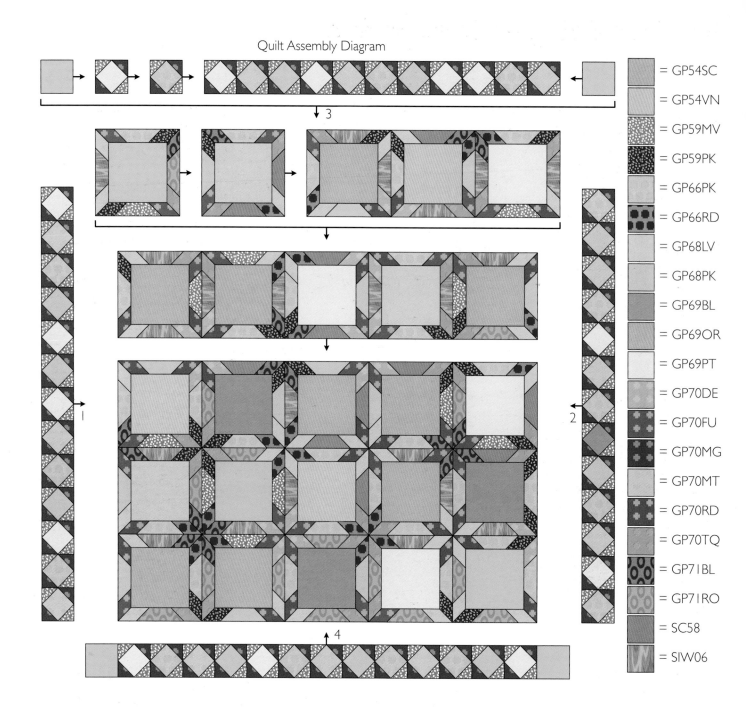

= GP54SC
= GP54VN
= GP59MV
= GP59PK
= GP66PK
= GP66RD
= GP68LV
= GP68PK
= GP69BL
= GP69OR
= GP69PT
= GP70DE
= GP70FU
= GP70MG
= GP70MT
= GP70RD
= GP70TQ
= GP71BL
= GP71RO
= SC58
= SIW06

together. Therefore for all the main blocks follow block assembly diagrams a and b. Get all the blocks to this stage, then using the inset seam method complete the blocks as shown in block assembly diagram c. The finished block can be seen in diagram d. Make 25 blocks.

MAKING THE BORDER BLOCKS
Refer to the quilt assembly diagram for fabric placement. Piece a total of 52 border blocks

following block assembly diagrams e and f. The finished border block can be seen in diagram g.

MAKING THE QUILT
Join the main blocks into 5 rows of 5 blocks, then join the rows to form the quilt centre. Stitch the border blocks into 4 rows of 13 blocks. Add a row to each side of the quilt centre, then join a corner post to each end of the remaining 2 rows. Finally add these to the top and bottom of the quilt centre.

FINISHING THE QUILT
Press the quilt top. Seam the backing pieces using a ¼in (6mm) seam allowance to form a piece approx. 83in x 83in (211cm x 211cm). Layer the quilt top, batting and backing and baste together (see page 138). Using pink machine quilting thread, quilt in the ditch in all the seams and on the large squares quilt squares, 1½in and 2½in (3.75cm and 6.25cm) from the seam. Trim the quilt edges and attach the binding (see page 139).

Red Star Bouquet Quilt ★★★

Kaffe Fassett

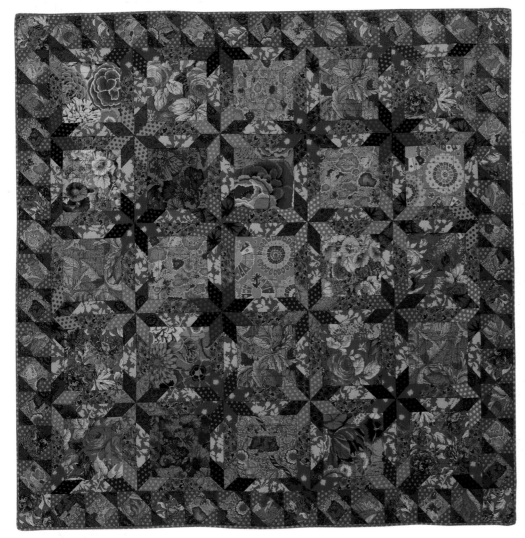

Looking for a new version of this quilt I settled on reds as there are so many in my new range. I'm excited about the interplay of polka dots and simpler fabrics with the richly detailed florals. These succulent reds, oranges and pinks should warm up any room.

SIZE OF QUILT
The finished quilt will measure approx. 75in x 75in (190.5cm x 190.5cm).

MATERIALS
Patchwork Fabrics:

BEKAH
Magenta	GP69MG: ⅜yd (35cm)

SPOT
Burgundy	GP70BG: ¼yd (25cm)
Black	GP70BK: ⅜yd (35cm)
Fuchsia	GP70FU: ⅜yd (35cm)
Green	GP70GN: ⅛yd (15cm)
Magenta	GP70MG: ¾yd (70cm)
Periwinkle	GP70PE: ⅛yd (15cm)
Purple	GP70PU: ¼yd (25cm)
Red	GP70RD: ⅛yd (15cm) or use leftover from binding.

ABORIGINAL DOTS
Periwinkle	GP71PE: ¼yd (25cm)

LICHEN
Rust	GP76RU: ⅝yd (60cm)

SILHOUETTE ROSE
Wine	GP77WN: ¾yd (70cm)

ANEMONE
Magenta	GP78MG: ¾yd (70cm)
Purple	GP78PU: ⅛yd (15cm)

TURKISH DELIGHT
Red	GP81RD: ⅜yd (35cm)

STENCIL CARNATION
Rose	GP82RO: ¼yd (25cm)

DANCING LEAVES
Gold	GP83GD: ½yd (45cm)
Heather	GP83HE: ⅜yd (35cm)

HERALDIC
Scarlet	GP84SC: ⅜yd (35cm)

WINDING FLORAL
Indigo	GP85IN: ¾yd (70cm)

GRANDIOSE
Rust	PJ13RU: ⅜yd (35cm)

BLOUSEY
Magenta	PJ15MG: ⅝yd (60cm)

TALL HOLLYHOCKS
Pink	PJ16PK: ⅜yd (35cm)

LILAC ROSE
Scarlet	PJ17SC: ⅜yd (35cm)

BEGONIA LEAVES
Magenta	PJ18MG: ¼yd (25cm)

PRINTED IKAT POLKADOT
Red	PKDRD: ⅜yd (35cm)

Backing Fabric: 5⅜yds (4.9m)
Any of the large floral prints in the quilt would be suitable for backing.

Binding:
SPOT
Red   GP70RD: ¾yd (70cm)

Batting:
83in × 83in (211cm × 211cm).

Quilting thread:
Dark red machine quilting thread.

Templates: See Pastel Star Bouquet Quilt.

PATCH SHAPES
See Pastel Star Bouquet Quilt instructions.

CUTTING OUT
Cut the fabric in the order stated to prevent waste.

Large Square: Cut 9½in (24.25cm) strips across the width of the fabric. Each strip will give you 4 patches per width. Cut 9½in (24.25cm) squares, cut 4 in GP69MG, PJ17SC, 3 in GP76RU, PJ15MG, 2 in GP81RD, GP83GD, GP83HE, PJ13RU, PJ16PK and 1 in GP84SC.

Border Corner Posts: Fussy cut 4 × 5½in (14cm) squares in PJ15MG.

Template H: Cut 2½ in (6.25cm) strips across the width of the fabric. Each strip will give you 6 patches per width. Cut 50 in GP77WN and GP78MG.

Template I: Cut 2½ in (6.25cm) strips across the width of the fabric. Each strip will give you 10 patches per width. Cut 25 in GP70BK, 24 in GP70FU, PKDRD, 17 in GP71PE, 16 in GP70BG, GP82RO, GP85IN, PJ18MG, 12 in GP70PU, 10 in GP78PU, 8 in GP70GN, GP70PE 6 in GP70MG and 2 in GP70RD.

Template J: Cut 3⅜in (8.5cm) strips across the width of the fabric. Each strip will give you 22 patches per width. Cut 104 in GP70MG and GP85IN.

Template K: Cut 4in (10.25cm) strips across the width of the fabric. Each strip will give you 10 patches per width. Cut 15 in GP76RU, 14 in GP83GD, 12 in GP84SC and 11 in PJ15MG.

Binding: Cut 8 strips 2½in (6.5cm) wide across the width of the fabric in GP70FU.

Backing: Cut 2 pieces 40in × 83in (101.5cm × 211cm), 2 pieces 40in × 4in (101.5cm × 10.25cm) and 1 piece 4in × 4in (10.25cm × 10.25cm) in backing fabric. Note: For a quirky look to the backing you could cut the 4in square from a different fabric and piece the backing with the contrasting square

in the centre.

MAKING THE MAIN BLOCKS
See Pastel Star Bouquet Quilt instructions.

MAKING THE BORDER BLOCKS
See Pastel Star Bouquet Quilt instructions.

MAKING THE QUILT
See Pastel Star Bouquet Quilt instructions.

FINISHING THE QUILT
See Pastel Star Bouquet Quilt instructions.
Note: Use dark red quilting thread for this version.

Quilt Assembly Diagram

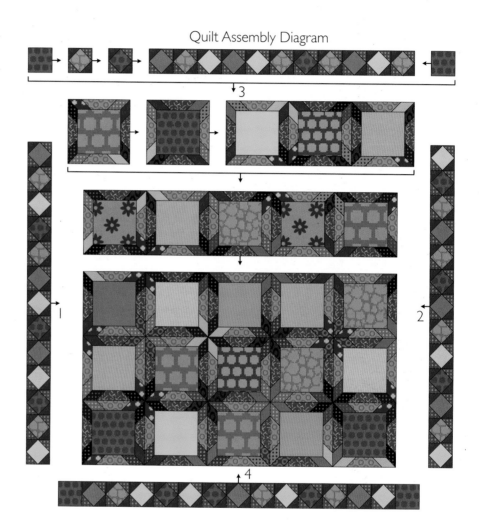

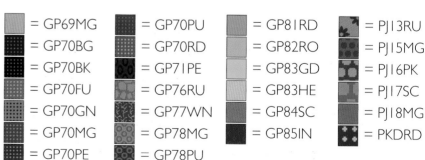

= GP69MG	= GP70PU
= GP70BG	= GP70RD
= GP70BK	= GP71PE
= GP70FU	= GP76RU
= GP70GN	= GP77WN
= GP70MG	= GP78MG
= GP70PE	= GP78PU

= GP81RD	= PJ13RU
= GP82RO	= PJ15MG
= GP83GD	= PJ16PK
= GP83HE	= PJ17SC
= GP84SC	= PJ18MG
= GP85IN	= PKDRD

Diagonal Madness Quilt ★★

KAFFE FASSETT

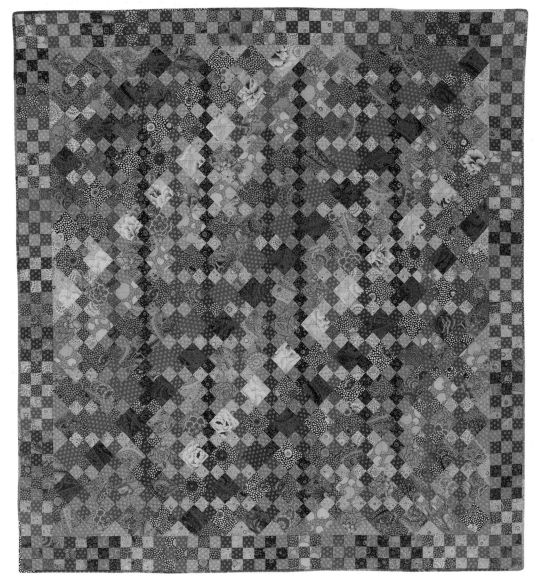

A vintage quilt in Mary Mashuta's book Cotton Candy Quilts was the starting point for this quilt.
I love the scrappiness of it and the strong diagonals that emerge while maintaining rippling vertical stripes, yet another amazing use of simple squares.

SIZE OF QUILT
The finished quilt will measure approx. 80in x 85in (203cm x 216cm).

MATERIALS
Patchwork Fabrics:
ROMAN GLASS
Byzantium	GP01BY:	⅜yd (35cm)
Pink	GP01PK:	⅝yd (60cm)
Pastel	GP01PT:	⅜yd (35cm)

PAPERWEIGHT
Gypsy	GP20GY:	⅜yd (35cm)

KIMONO
Lavender Blue	GP33LB:	¼yd (25cm)

CLOISONNE
Terracotta	GP46TC:	⅝yd (60cm)

FLOWER BASKET
Magenta	GP48MG:	½yd (45cm)

FLOATING FLOWERS
Pastel	GP56PT:	½yd (45cm)

GUINEA FLOWER
Pink	GP59PK:	1yd (90cm)
White	GP59WH:	½yd (45cm)
Yellow	GP59YE:	½yd (45cm)

PAISLEY JUNGLE
Green	GP60GN:	½yd (45cm)
Rust	GP60RU:	½yd (45cm)
Tangerine	GP60TN:	¾yd (70cm)

PINKING FLOWER
Gold	GP66GD:	½yd (45cm)

SPOT
Fuchsia	GP70FU:	⅝yd (60cm)
Magenta	GP70MG:	¾yd (70cm)
Mint	GP70MT:	½yd (45cm)
Pink	GP70PK:	⅛yd (15cm)
Red	GP70RD:	⅝yd (60cm)

Turquoise   GP70TQ: ¾yd (70cm)
ABORIGINAL DOTS
Blue   GP71BL: ½yd (45cm)

Backing Fabric: 7¾yds (7.1m)
We suggest these fabrics for backing:
GUINEA FLOWER Pink, GP59PK
PAISLEY JUNGLE Green, GP60GN
Note: Leftover backing fabric can be used in the quilt.

Binding:
The binding was pieced from leftover patchwork fabrics.

Batting:
88in × 93in (223.5cm × 236cm).
Quilting thread:
Perlé embroidery thread in cerise pink.
Templates:

K   Q   R   J

PATCH SHAPES
The centre section of this quilt is made of 4 patch blocks using 1 square patch shape (Template Q) alternated with a second square patch shape (Template K). These are set 'on point' into diagonal rows and the edges and corners of the centre are completed with 2 triangle patch shapes (Templates J and R). The centre section is surrounded with a border pieced from 9 patch blocks, using the same square patch shape as the 4 patch blocks (Template Q).

CUTTING OUT
Cut the fabric in the order stated to prevent waste, trim leftover strips for later templates as appropriate.
Template J: Cut 3⅜in (8.5cm) strips across the width of the fabric. Cut 4 in GP70TQ.
Template K: Cut 4in (10.25cm) strips across the width of the fabric. Each strip will give you 10 patches per width. Cut 32 in GP46TC, 27 in GP60GN, GP60RU, 19 in GP60TN, 18 in GP33LB, GP59YE, 16 in GP59PK, GP59WH, 15 in GP66GD, 13 in GP70FU, 8 in GP48MG and 1 in GP70MG.
Template Q: Cut 2¼in (5.75cm) strips across the width of the fabric. Each strip will give you 17 patches per width. Cut 123 in GP59PK, 120 in GP70MG, 117 in GP70TQ, 109 in GP70RD, 89 in GP01PK, 74 in GP01BY, 70 in GP70MT, 68 in GP56PT, GP70FU, 65 in GP20GY, 64 in GP71BL, 60 in GP60TN, 55 in GP01PT, 50 in GP48MG, 35 in GP59YE, 34 in GP66GD, 20 in GP59WH, 18 in GP46TC and 11 in GP70PK (Total 1250 squares).
Template R: Cut 3⅛in (8cm) strips across the width of the fabric. Each strip will give you 12 patches per width. Cut 10 in GP70MT, 9 in GP60TN, 8 in GP01PK, 6 in GP56PT, GP59PK, GP70TQ, GP71BL and 3 in GP48MG.

Binding: Cut a total of 9½ yards (8.7m) of 2½in (6.5cm) wide binding from leftover patchwork fabric.

Backing: Cut 2 pieces 40in × 88in (101.5cm × 223.5cm) and 1 piece 14in × 88in (35.5cm × 223.5cm) in backing fabric.

MAKING THE QUILT CENTRE
Use a ¼in (6mm) seam allowance throughout. Refer to the quilt assembly diagram for fabric placement. Piece a total of 182 4 patch blocks as shown in the 4 patch block assembly diagrams a and b. The finished block can be seen in diagram c. Lay the blocks out as shown in the quilt assembly diagram, alternating with the template K squares. Add the template R and J triangles to complete the edges and corners of the centre. Carefully separate into diagonal rows

4 Patch Block Assembly Diagrams

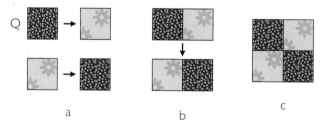

a   b   c

9 Patch Block Assembly Diagrams

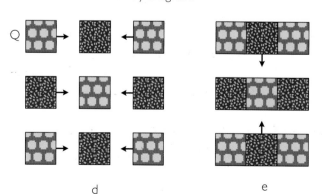

d   e   f

and join. Join the rows to complete the quilt centre.

ADDING THE BORDERS
Refer to the quilt assembly diagram for fabric placement. Piece a total of 58 9 patch blocks as shown in the 9 patch block assembly diagrams d and e. The finished block can be seen in diagram f. Piece the blocks into 2 strips of 14 blocks for the quilt sides and 2 strips of 15 blocks for the quilt top and bottom. Note: You may need to add an extra 3 squares to the ends of your borders and then trim to fit exactly as they may be a little short. When Pauline stitched the sample quilt, by some miracle they actually fitted, which they shouldn't have done! Add the borders to the quilt centre as shown in the quilt assembly diagram.

FINISHING THE QUILT
Press the quilt top. Seam the backing pieces using a ¼in (6mm) seam allowance to form a piece approx. 88in x 93in (223.5cm x 236cm). Layer the quilt top, batting and backing and baste together (see page 138). Using cerise pink perlé embroidery thread quilt a cross hatch pattern vertically and horizontally through the template K and 4 patch blocks. In the 9 patch border blocks quilt diagonally through each block to form X shapes. Trim the quilt edges and attach the binding (see page 139).

Quilt Assembly Diagram

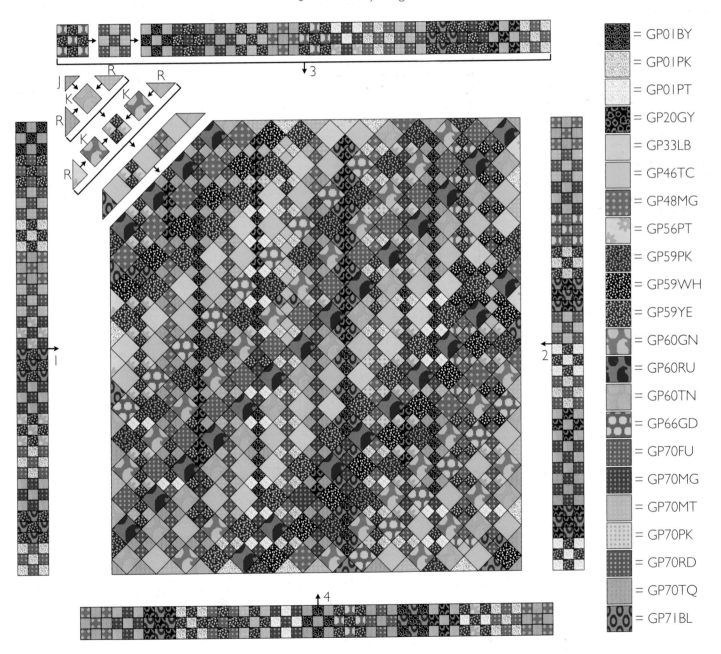

= GP01BY
= GP01PK
= GP01PT
= GP20GY
= GP33LB
= GP46TC
= GP48MG
= GP56PT
= GP59PK
= GP59WH
= GP59YE
= GP60GN
= GP60RU
= GP60TN
= GP66GD
= GP70FU
= GP70MG
= GP70MT
= GP70PK
= GP70RD
= GP70TQ
= GP71BL

Garden Whirligig Quilt ★★★

MARY MASHUTA

I'm not a gardener: I just admire. Now with Kaffe's fabrics I have created my own garden complete with whimsical garden ornaments.

SIZE OF QUILT
The finished quilt will measure approx. 78in × 78in (198cm × 198cm).

MATERIALS
Patchwork Fabrics:
SPOT

Burgundy	GP70BG: ¼yd (25cm)
Duck Egg	GP70DE: ⅜yd (35cm)
Fuchsia	GP70FU: ⅜yd (35cm)
Magenta	GP70MG: ¼yd (25cm)
Mint	GP70MT: ⅜yd (35cm)
Periwinkle	GP70PE: ⅜yd (35cm)
Red	GP70RD: ⅜yd (35cm)
Taupe	GP70TA: 2¼yds (2.1m)
Turquoise	GP70TQ: ⅜yd (35cm)
Yellow	GP70YE: ⅜yd (35cm)

Appliqué Fabrics:
ZINNIA

Magenta	GP31MG: ¼yd (25cm)
Sky Blue or Pink	GP31SK or PK: ¼yd (25cm)

Border and Sashing Fabrics:
JUNGLE STRIPE

Autumn	GP65AT: 1½yds (1.4m)

TARGETS

Pastel	GP67PT: ¼yd (25cm)

BEKAH

Magenta	GP69MG: ⅜yd (35cm)
Orange	GP69OR: 2yds (1.8m)

Backing Fabric: 5¾yds (5.3m)
We suggest these fabrics for backing:
TARGETS Red,   GP67RD
TARGETS   Brown, GP67BR
TARGETS Contrast, GP67CO

Binding:
WOVEN HAZE STRIPE
Raspberry   HZS12: ¾yd (70cm)

Batting:
86in × 86in (218.5cm × 218.5cm).

Quilting thread:
Toning and gold machine quilting threads.

Templates:

PATCH SHAPES
The 'Whirligig' blocks which finish to 10in
(25.5cm) are pieced from 3 patch shapes
(Templates T, U and V) each also has a circle
(Template W) appliquéd to form the centre
of the block. The blocks are then straight set,
interspaced with sashing strips and posts (cut
to size). The centre is surrounded by a
border with corner posts (cut to size).

CUTTING OUT
Refer to the cutting diagrams before cutting
templates T, U and V. The layouts show the
most economical way to cut a width strip of
patch shapes.
Template T: Cut 4½in (11.5cm) strips across
the width of the fabric. Each strip will give
you 13 patches per width. Cut 100 in
GP70TA.
Template V: Cut 4½in (11.5cm) strips across
the width of the fabric. Each strip will give
you 15 patches per width. Cut 100 in
GP70TA.
Template U: Cut 4½in (11.5cm) strips across
the width of the fabric. Each strip will give
you 11 patches per width. Cut 13 in
GP70FU, GP70PE, GP70RD, 12 in GP70DE,
GP70MT, GP70TQ, GP70YE, 9 in GP70MG, 4
in GP70BG.
Template W: Fussy cut 3in (7.5cm) circles
centring on the flowers in the fabric. Cut 13
in GP31SK or PK and 12 in GP31MG.
Sashing Strips: Cut 3½in (9cm) strips across
the width of the fabric. Each strip will give
you 3 patches per width. Cut 3½in × 10½in
(9cm × 26.75cm) rectangles. Cut 40 in
GP65AT.

Block Assembly Diagrams

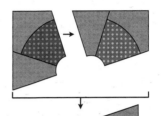

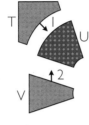

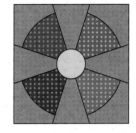

a

b

c

Cutting Diagrams

Quilt Assembly Diagram

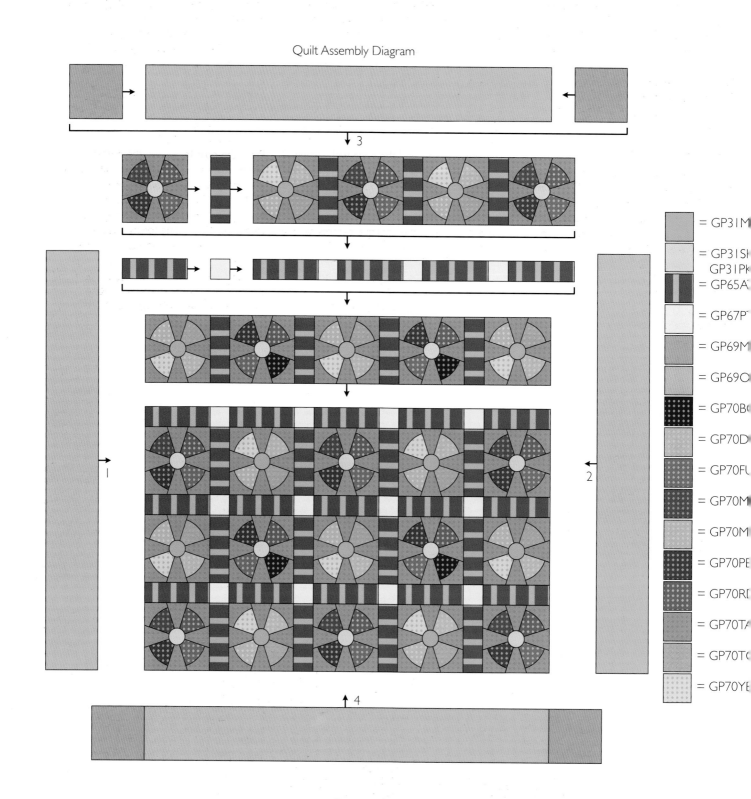

= GP31M

= GP31Sł
  GP31Pk

= GP65A

= GP67P

= GP69M

= GP69O

= GP70B

= GP70D

= GP70FL

= GP70M

= GP70M

= GP70PE

= GP70RD

= GP70TA

= GP70TC

= GP70YE

Sashing Posts: Cut 3½in (9cm) strips across the width of the fabric. Each strip will give you 11 patches per width. Cut 3½in (9cm) squares. Cut 16 in GP67PT.

Borders: Cut from the length of the fabric cut 4 borders 62½in x 8½in (158.75cm x 21.5cm) in GP69OR.

Border Corner Posts: Cut 4 x 8½in (21.5cm) squares in GP69MG.

Binding: Cut 9yds (8.25m) of 2½in (6.5cm) wide bias binding in HZS12.

Backing: Cut 2 pieces 40in x 86in (101.5cm x 218.5cm) in backing fabric, 2 pieces 40in x 7in (101.5cm x 17.75cm) and 1 piece 7in x 7in (17.75cm x 17.75cm) in backing fabric. Note: For a quirky look to the backing you could cut the 7in (17.75cm) square from a different fabric and piece the backing with the contrasting square in the centre.

MAKING THE BLOCKS

Use a ¼in (6mm) seam allowance throughout. Refer to the quilt assembly diagram for fabric placement. First piece the template T shapes to the template U shapes using the curved seam method shown in the Patchwork Know How section at the back of the book. Next add a template V shape as shown in block assembly diagram a. Make 4 for each block. Piece the 4 sections together as shown in diagram b.

APPLIQUÉ

Cut out a 2½in (6.25cm) circle in stiff card. Take a template W fabric circle and work a running stitch around the edge with strong thread. Place the card circle in the centre of the reverse of the circle and pull up the stitching to gather the shape. Press with the card circle in place, then remove the card circle. This makes the appliqué centres for the blocks. Appliqué a centre to each block, the darker GP31MG centres go on the lighter blocks and the lighter GP31SK or PK centres go on the darker blocks. This can be done by hand or machine using a blanket stitch to secure the edge.

MAKING THE QUILT

Join the blocks into 5 rows of 5 blocks interspacing with sashing strips, also make 4 rows of sashing strips and posts as shown in the quilt assembly diagram. Join the rows to form the quilt centre. Add the side borders to the quilt centre. Join a corner post to each end of the top and bottom borders then add to the quilt centre to complete the quilt.

FINISHING THE QUILT

Press the quilt top. Seam the backing pieces using a ¼in (6mm) seam allowance to form a piece approx. 86in x 86in (218.5cm x 218.5cm). Layer the quilt top, batting and backing and baste together (see page 138). Using toning machine quilting thread, quilt in the ditch of the sashing and border seams only. Using gold thread, quilt the blocks, sashing, borders and corner posts as shown in the quilting diagram. Trim the quilt edges and attach the binding (see page 139).

Quilting Diagram

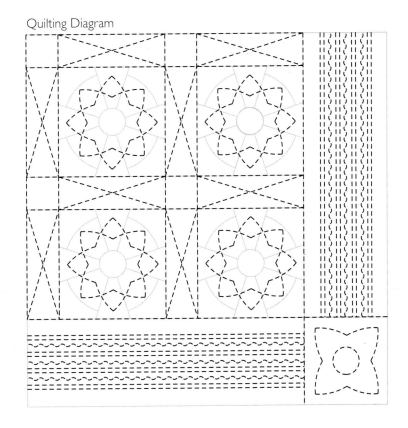

Windmills Quilt ★★

PAULINE SMITH

The brightly coloured windmills Pauline uses as bird scarers in her garden set against the hot colours of a late summer flower border gave her the idea for this quilt.

SIZE OF QUILT
The finished quilt will measure approx. 73in x 61in (185.5cm x 155cm).

MATERIALS
Patchwork Fabrics:
PAPERWEIGHT
Paprika   GP20PP: ¼yd (25cm)
ZINNIA
Crimson   GP31CR: ⅜yd (35cm)
FLOATING FLOWERS
Blue   GP56BL: ½yd (45cm)
PAPER FANS
Red   GP57RD: ½yd (45cm)
Teal   GP57TE: ⅜yd (35cm)
PAISLEY JUNGLE
Purple   GP60PU: ¼yd (25cm)

POTENTILLA
Red   GP64RD: 1⅛yds (1m)
                       includes borders
JUNGLE STRIPE
Dark   GP65DK: ¾yd (70cm)
Red   GP65RD: ⅜yd (35cm)
PINKING FLOWER
Red   GP66RD: ⅜yd (35cm)
SPOT
Fuchsia   GP70FU: ¼yd (25cm)
Magenta   GP70MG: ¼yd (25cm)
Red   GP70RD: ¼yd (25cm)
ABORIGINAL DOTS
Rose   GP71RO: ¼yd (25cm)
WOVEN HAZE STRIPE
Sunshine   HZS06: ¼yd (25cm)

CORAL LEAF
Sage   PJ12SA: ¾yd (70cm)
                       includes borders

Backing Fabric: 4⅛yds (3.8m)
We suggest these fabrics for backing:
FLORAL STRIPE Purple, GP62PU
PAISLEY JUNGLE Purple, GP60PU
POTENTILLA Red, GP64RD

Binding:
JUNGLE STRIPE
Dark   GP65DK: ⅝yd (60cm)

Batting:
80in x 69in (203cm x 175cm).

Block Assembly Diagrams

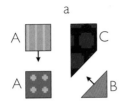
a

b

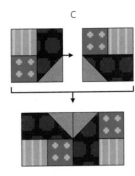
c

Quilting thread:
Scarlet machine quilting thread.

Templates:

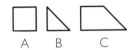

A   B   C

PATCH SHAPES
This interesting windmill block which finishes to 12in (30.5cm) uses 3 patch shapes. I square (Template A) I triangle (Template B) and a lozenge patch shape (Template C). The block is pieced into 4 identical quarters which are then rotated and joined to produce the windmill block. The blocks are straight set into rows and then surrounded with an inner and outer border, both with corner posts, cut to size.

CUTTING OUT
Cut the fabric in the order stated to prevent waste.
Outer Border Corner Posts: Cut 4 x 4½in (11.5cm) squares in GP57RD, reserve the remaining fabric and trim for template A.
Template A: Cut 3½in (9cm) strips across the width of the fabric. Each strip will give you 11 patches per width. Cut 28 in GP57RD, 24 in GP66RD, 20 in GP71RO, 16 in GP70MG, HZS06, 12 in GP20PP, GP64RD, GP70FU, GP70RD and 8 in PJ12SA.
Template B: Cut 3⅞in (9.75cm) strips across the width of the fabric. Each strip will give you 20 patches per width. Cut 52 in GP56BL and 28 in GP57TE.
Template C: Fabrics GP65DK and GP65RD have stripes which run the length of the fabric. These were fussy cut to utilize the individual design elements, with some running vertically and some running horizontally.

Refer to the photograph for help with this.
Fabric GP65DK Horizontal striped patches: Cut I strip 10¼in (26cm) wide down the length of the fabric, from this cut 6 strips 10¼in x 3½in (26cm x 9cm). Match the template to one square end of the strip and cut I patch shape. The opposite end forms a second patch shape, but check it is accurate by rotating the template 180 degrees. Cut 12.
Fabric GP65DK Vertical striped patches: Using the remaining fabric cut 3½in (9cm) strips down the length of the fabric, fussy cutting the strips on the fabric stripes. Using the template in the same way as before cut 24. Fabric GP65RD: Using the same techniques cut 8 patches with vertical and 8 patches with horizontal stripes.
Template C: Other fabrics. Cut 3½in (9cm) strips across the width of the fabric. Each

strip will give you 7 patches per width. Cut 16 in GP31CR and 12 in GP60PU.
Inner border Corner Posts: Cut 4 x 3in (7.5cm) squares in GP64RD.
Inner Border: Cut 6 strips 3in (7.5cm) wide x the width of the fabric. Join as necessary and cut 2 strips 60½in x 3in (153.75cm x 7.5cm) for the quilt sides and 2 strips 48½in x 3in (123.25cm x 7.5cm) for the quilt top and bottom in PJ12SA.
Outer Border: Cut 6 strips 4½in (11.5cm) wide x the width of the fabric. Join as necessary and cut 2 strips 65½in x 4½in (166.5cm x 11.5cm) for the quilt sides and 2 strips 53½in x 4½in (136cm x 11.5cm) for the quilt top and bottom in GP64RD.

Binding: Cut 7 strips 2½in (6.5cm) wide across the width of the fabric in GP65DK.

Quilting Diagram

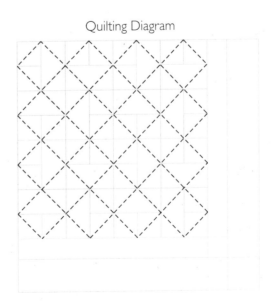

Backing: Cut 2 pieces 40in x 69in (101.5cm x 175cm) in backing fabric.

MAKING THE BLOCKS

Use a ¼in (6mm) seam allowance throughout. Refer to the quilt assembly diagram and photograph for fabric placement. Each block is made of 4 identical quarters. Follow block assembly diagrams a and b to make 4 identical quarters per block. Then join the quarters to form the block as

shown in diagram c. Make 20 blocks.

MAKING THE QUILT

Join the blocks into 5 rows of 4 blocks, then join the rows to form the quilt centre. Add the side inner borders to the quilt centre. Join a corner post to each end of the top and bottom inner borders then add to the quilt centre. Join the outer borders in the same way to complete the quilt.

FINISHING THE QUILT

Press the quilt top. Seam the backing pieces using a ¼in (6mm) seam allowance to form a piece approx. 80in x 69in (203cm x 175cm). Layer the quilt top, batting and backing and baste together (see page 138). Using scarlet machine quilting thread, quilt a crosshatching pattern diagonally though the quilt centre as shown in the quilting diagram. Trim the quilt edges and attach the binding (see page 139).

Quilt Assembly Diagram

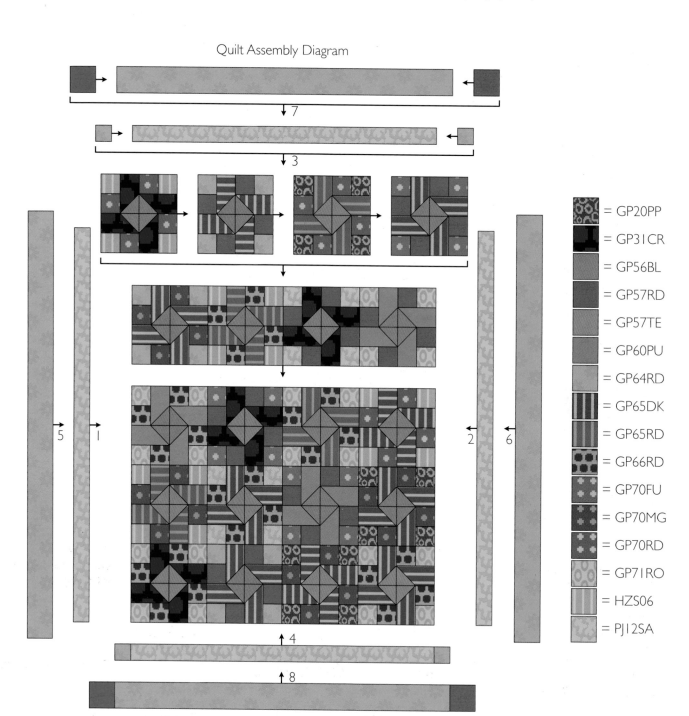

= GP20PP
= GP31CR
= GP56BL
= GP57RD
= GP57TE
= GP60PU
= GP64RD
= GP65DK
= GP65RD
= GP66RD
= GP70FU
= GP70MG
= GP70RD
= GP71RO
= HZS06
= PJ12SA

Right on Target Quilt ★★

SALLY DAVIS

Sally's quilt would make a great gift for a student off to college. It would be easy to use the layout and take one of the other colourways of Targets as a starting point to create your own version.

SIZE OF QUILT
The finished quilt will measure approx. 82in × 64in (208cm × 162.5cm).

MATERIALS
Patchwork Fabrics:
PAPERWEIGHT
Lime   GP20LM: ¼yd (25cm)
TARGETS
Pastel   GP67PT: 3yds (2.75m)
SPOT
Fuchsia   GP70FU: ¼yd (25cm)

Periwinkle   GP70PE: ¼yd (25cm)
Turquoise   GP70TQ: ¼yd (25cm)
Yellow   GP70YE: ¼yd (25cm)
ABORIGINAL DOTS
Gold   GP71GD: ¼yd (25cm)
SHOT COTTON
Tangerine   SC11: ¼yd (25cm)
Lavender   SC14: ¼yd (25cm)
Apple   SC39: ¼yd (25cm)
Lime   SC43: 1½yds (1.4m)
includes binding.
Forget–Me–Not   SC51: ¼yd (25cm)

Backing Fabric: 5⅜yds (4.9m)
Any of the SPOT fabrics used in the quilt would be suitable for backing.

Binding:
SHOT COTTON
Lime   SC43:
                See patchwork fabrics.

Batting:
90in × 72in (228.5cm × 183cm).

Quilting thread:
Toning machine quilting thread.

Templates:

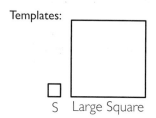

S Large Square

PATCH SHAPES

Freeform long cabin blocks which are built around a square patch shape (Template S) are alternated with large squares (cut to size) of Targets fabric. The quilt is finished with a narrow inner border and a wider outer border. The diagram for this quilt shows fabric placement accurately, but not the varied log widths, so refer to the photograph for more help.

CUTTING OUT

Cut the fabric in the order stated to prevent waste, please cut the TARGETS fabric (GP67PT) carefully, refer to the cutting diagram for GP67PT.

Outer Border: From the length of the fabric cut 2 strips 4½in x 74½in (11.5cm x 189.25cm) for the sides of the quilt and 2 strips 4½in x 64½in (11.5cm x 163.75cm) for the top and bottom of the quilt.

Large Squares: Cut a total of 24 x 9½in (24.25) squares. Reserve the remaining fabric for log cabin blocks.

Inner Borders: Cut 7 strips 1½in (3.75cm) wide across the width of fabric in SC43. Join as necessary and cut 2 strips 1½in x 72½in (3.75cm x 184.25cm) for the sides of the quilt and 2 strips 1½in x 56½in (3.75cm x 143.5cm) for the top and bottom of the quilt.

Binding: Cut 8 strips 2½in (6.5cm) wide across the width of the fabric in SC43. Reserve the remaining fabric for log cabin blocks.

Log Cabin Blocks;

Template S: For the log cabin centres cut a total of 24 x 2in (5cm) squares from patchwork fabrics. From the remaining fabrics cut strips for the log cabin blocks. The widths of these strips are 1in, 1¼in, 1½in 1¾in and 2in (2.5cm, 3.25cm, 3.75cm, 4.5cm and 5cm). We suggest cutting strips and piecing as you go for these blocks as each 'round' of logs should be pieced from the same fabric and width of strip.

Backing: Cut 1 piece 40in x 90in (101.5cm x 228.5cm) and 1 piece 33in x 90in (84cm x 228.5cm) in backing fabric.

MAKING THE BLOCKS

Use a ¼in (6mm) seam allowance throughout. The diagram for this quilt shows fabric placement accurately, but not the varied log widths, so refer to the photograph for more help. Piece a total of 24 log cabin blocks, the 'logs' are added to the block centre (template S squares) as shown in the log cabin diagram and trimmed to fit as you go. Use a single fabric and strip width for each round of 'logs'. Aim for the blocks to be about 10in (25.5cm) square. Then trim evenly to exactly 9½in (24.25cm) square.

MAKING THE QUILT

Lay out the trimmed log cabin blocks alternated with the large squares as shown in the quilt assembly diagram. Join into 8 rows of 6 blocks then join the rows to form the quilt centre. Add the side, then top and bottom inner borders as indicated in the

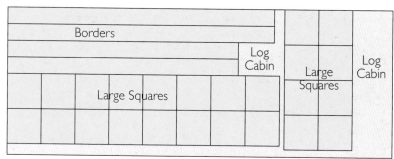

Cutting Diagram for GP67PT

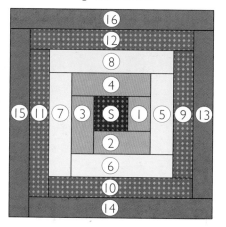

Log Cabin Block

quilt assembly diagram. Finally add the side, then top and bottom outer borders to complete the quilt.

FINISHING THE QUILT
Press the quilt top. Seam the backing pieces using a ¼in (6mm) seam allowance to form a piece approx. 90in × 72in (228.5cm × 183cm). Layer the quilt top, batting and backing and baste together (see page 138). Using toning machine quilting thread, stitch a wavy line pattern working along the log cabin 'logs' from the centre of each block to the outside. Then quilt the large squares and borders in a meander pattern following the pattern of the targets quilt to make spirals and curves in the quilting design. Trim the quilt edges and attach the binding (see page 139).

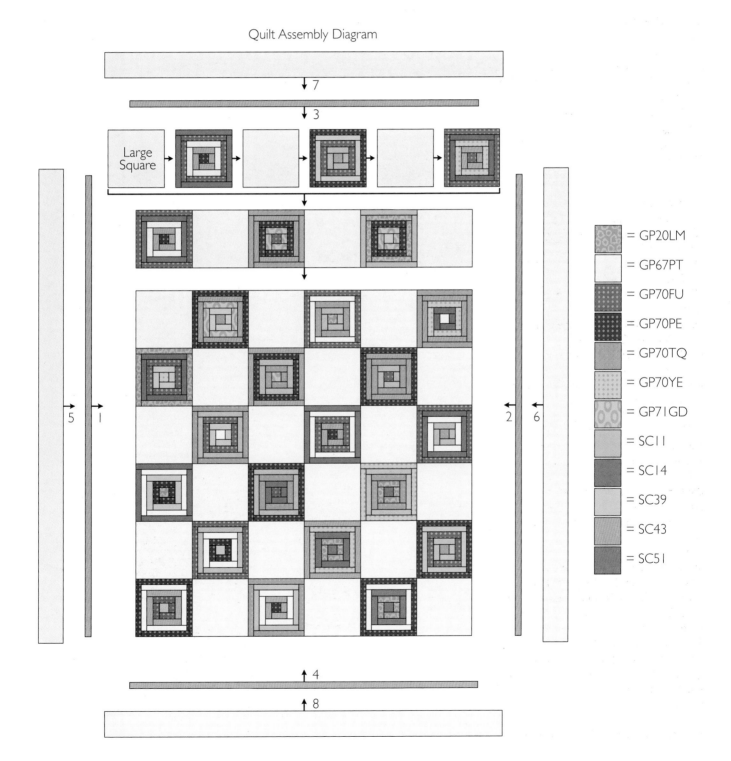

Quilt Assembly Diagram

= GP20LM
= GP67PT
= GP70FU
= GP70PE
= GP70TQ
= GP70YE
= GP71GD
= SC11
= SC14
= SC39
= SC43
= SC51

The Gift Quilt ★★★

BRANDON MABLY

Inspired by the Shaker song 'Tis A Gift To Be Simple' Brandon's quilt is a perfect gift for a newborn baby and would also be ideal for a floor cushion project.

SIZE OF QUILT
The finished quilt will measure approx.
33in x 27in (84cm x 68.5cm).

MATERIALS
Patchwork and Appliqué Fabrics:
JUNGLE STRIPE
Yellow   GP65YE: ½yd (45cm)

PINKING FLOWER
Gold   GP66GD: ⅛yd (15cm)
Pink   GP66PK: ⅛yd (15cm)
TARGETS
Red   GP67RD: ½yd (45cm)
BEKAH
Pastel   GP69PT: ⅛yd (15cm)

SPOT
Fuchsia   GP70FU: ½yd (45cm)
Mint   GP70MT: ⅛yd (15cm)
Periwinkle   GP70PE: ⅛yd (15cm)
Turquoise   GP70TQ: ⅛yd (15cm)
Backing Fabric: 1yd (90cm)
We suggest these fabrics for backing:

PINKING FLOWER Pink, GP66PK
BEKAH Pastel, GP69PT
SPOT Mint, GP70MT

Binding:
WOVEN HAZE STRIPE
Persimmon   HZS01: ⅜yd (35cm)

Batting:
40in x 34in (101.5cm x 86.5cm).

Quilting Thread:
Hand quilting thread in salmon pink

Other Materials:
Lightweight adhesive web

Template:

A

PATCH SHAPES
The quilt is formed using one square patch shape (Template A) which is used to 4 piece sections. Each section then has borders (cut to size) added on 2 sides. The 4 sections are interspaced with sashing strips (cut to size). The appliqué is then added using adhesive web and stitched into place. Note, the appliqué shapes on page 134 & 135 are printed at 50% of real size, to use scale them

Quilt Assembly Diagram

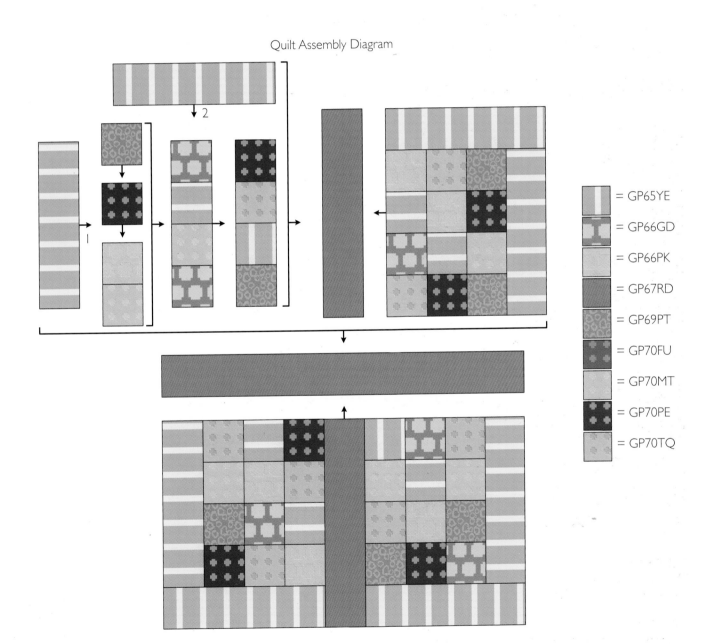

= GP65YE
= GP66GD
= GP66PK
= GP67RD
= GP69PT
= GP70FU
= GP70MT
= GP70PE
= GP70TQ

up 200% on a photocopier. The shapes are already reversed to make tracing onto adhesive web simple, the shapes also have dotted line sections which are where the shapes are layered.

CUTTING OUT

Sashing: Cut 1 sashing strip 27½in x 3½in (69.75cm x 9cm) and 2 strips 15½in x 3½in (39.5cm x 9cm) in GP67RD.

Borders: Cut 8 strips 12½in x 3½in (31.75cm x 9cm) in GP65YE.

Template A: Cut 3½in (9cm) wide strips across the width of the fabric. Each strip will give you 11 patches per width. Cut 8 in GP65YE, GP70TQ, 7 in GP69PT, GP70PE, 6 in GP66GD, GP66PK and GP70MT.

Appliqué Shapes: Scale up the appliqué shapes to the correct size. Trace the shapes onto the paper side of your adhesive web leaving a ¼in (6mm) gap between the shapes. Roughly cut out the motifs about ⅛in (3mm) outside your drawn line. Bond the shapes to REVERSE of the fabrics. Use GP67RD for appliqué shapes 1 and 2, use GP70FU for shapes 3, 4, 5, 6 and 7. Place to one side until the piecing is complete.

Binding: Cut 3¾yds (3.4m) of 2½in (6.5cm) wide bias binding in HZS01.

Backing: Cut 1 piece 40in x 34in (101.5cm x 86.5cm) in backing fabric.

MAKING THE QUILT

Use a ¼in (6mm) seam allowance throughout. Referring to the quilt assembly diagram for fabric placement piece 4 sections using the template A squares. Add borders to 2 sides of each section as shown, then piece the top 2 sections together inserting a sashing strip between. Repeat with the bottom 2 sections. Piece the top and bottom sections together inserting sashing strip between to complete the quilt.

ADDING THE APPLIQUÉ

Refer to the Machine Appliqué section in the Patchwork Know How at the end of the book for extra help. Cut out the appliqué shapes with very sharp scissors on the drawn line. Remove the backing papers and arrange the pieces as shown in the appliqué diagram. The pieces have dotted line areas which are

layered, these areas sit behind other shapes. Once all the shapes are correctly positioned bond into place. Stitch using a dark pink thread and a blanket stitch or close zigzag stitch. The stitching should sit mostly on the bonded shape.

Stitching order is as follows: Upper curve of shape 1, lower curve of shape 1, upper and lower curves of shape 3. Upper curve of shape 2, lower curve of shape 2, upper and lower curves of shape 4. Sides and bottom of shapes 5 and 6. Finally stitch all around shape 7.

FINISHING THE QUILT

Press the quilt top. Layer the quilt top, batting and backing and baste together (see page 138). Using Salmon pink hand quilting thread echo quilt the appliqué shapes about ¼in outside the shapes, Then stitch a simple cross hatching pattern diagonally in both directions in the background, extending the stitching across the borders, but avoiding the sashing and appliqué. Trim the quilt edges and attach the binding (see page 139).

Appliqué Diagram

Blooms Quilt ★★

PAULINE SMITH

Pauline has made her blooms from a simple block. To make each flowerhead distinct careful grouping of tones is important, the finishing touch is added by quilting petal shapes on each flower.

SIZE OF QUILT
The finished quilt will measure approx. 52in × 46in (132cm × 117cm).

MATERIALS
Patchwork Fabrics:
LOTUS LEAF
Wine   GP29WN: ¼yd (25cm)
DAHLIA BLOOMS
Lush   GP54LS: ⅜yd (35cm)

FLOATING FLOWERS
Blue   GP56BL: ⅜yd (35cm)
PAPER FANS
Teal   GP57TE: ¼yd (25cm)
VERBENA
Red   GP61RD: ¼yd (25cm)
POTENTILLA
Red   GP64RD: ⅜yd (35cm)
PINKING FLOWER
Red   GP66RD: ⅜yd (35cm)

BEKAH
Green   GP69GN: ½yd (45cm)
Magenta   GP69MG: ¾yd (70cm)
Orange   GP69OR: ¾yd (70cm)
ABORIGINAL DOTS
Blue   GP71BL: 1¼yds (1.15cm)

Backing Fabric: 3¼yds (3m)
We suggest these fabrics for backing:
POTENTILLA Red, GP64RD

BEKAH Magenta, GP69MG
BEKAH Orange, GP69OR

Binding:
BEKAH
Orange   GP69OR: ⅝yd (60cm)

Batting:
60in x 54in (152.5cm x 137.25cm).

Quilting thread:
Dark red machine quilting thread.

Templates:

PATCH SHAPES
This simple block uses 2 square patch shapes
(Templates A and U). The small squares (U)
are placed over 2 opposite corners of the
large squares (A) and stitched diagonally.
They are then trimmed and flipped back to
replace the corners of the large square.
These blocks are then pieced in fours to
make each larger 'Bloom' block. The 'Bloom'
blocks are then straight set into rows and
surrounded with a simple border to
complete the quilt.

CUTTING OUT
Template A: Cut 3½in (9cm) strips across
the width of the fabric. Each strip will give
you 11 patches per width. Cut 64 in
GP69OR, 56 in GP69MG, 28 in GP54LS, 24
in GP64RD, GP66RD, 16 in GP29WN and
12 in GP61RD
Template U: Cut 2in (5cm) strips across the
width of the fabric. Each strip will give you 20
patches per width. Cut 108 in GP69GN, 84
in GP56BL and 32 in GP57TE.
Borders: Cut 5 strips 2½in (3.75cm) wide
across the width of fabric in GP71BL. Join as
necessary and cut 2 strips 2½in x 52½in
(6.5cm x 133.5cm) for the sides of the quilt
and 2 strips 2½in x 42½in (6.5cm x 108cm)
for the top and bottom of the quilt.

Binding: Cut 6 strips 2½in (6.5cm) wide
across the width of the fabric in GP69OR.

Backing: Cut 1 piece 40in x 54in (101.5cm x
137.25cm) and 1 piece 21in x 54in (53.5cm
x 137.25cm) in backing fabric.

MAKING THE BLOCKS
Using the photograph as a guide sort the

Block Assembly Diagrams

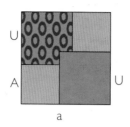

a

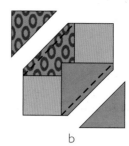

b

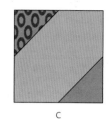

c

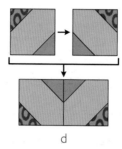

d

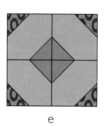

e

Quilting Diagram

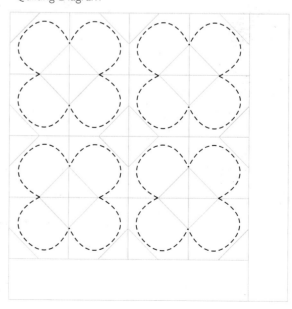

template A squares into groups of 4 with similar tones to make each 'Bloom' block. For each 'Bloom' block the 4 small squares which form the flower centre are the same fabric. Working on one set at a time take one large square (template A) and two small squares (template U), using the quilt assembly diagram as a guide to fabric combinations. Place one small square, right sides together onto 2 opposite corners of the large square, matching the edges carefully as shown in block assembly diagram a. Stitch diagonally across the small squares as shown in diagram

b. Trim the corners to a ¼in (6mm) seam allowance and press the corners out (diagram c). Make 4 for each 'Bloom' block.

Using a ¼in (6mm) seam allowance throughout join the 4 squares to form the 'Bloom' block as shown in diagram d, the finished block can be seen in diagram e. Make 56 'Bloom' blocks.

MAKING THE QUILT CENTRE
Piece the blocks into 8 rows of 7 blocks then join the rows to form the quilt centre. Add

the borders in the order indicated in the quilt assembly diagram.

FINISHING THE QUILT
Press the quilt top. Seam the backing pieces using a ¼in (6mm) seam allowance to form a piece approx 60in x 54in (152.5cm x 137.25cm). Layer the quilt top, batting and backing and baste together (see page 138). Using dark red machine quilting thread quilt flower petal shapes in each 'Bloom' block as shown in the quilting diagram. Trim the quilt edges and attach the binding (see page 139).

Quilt Assembly Diagram

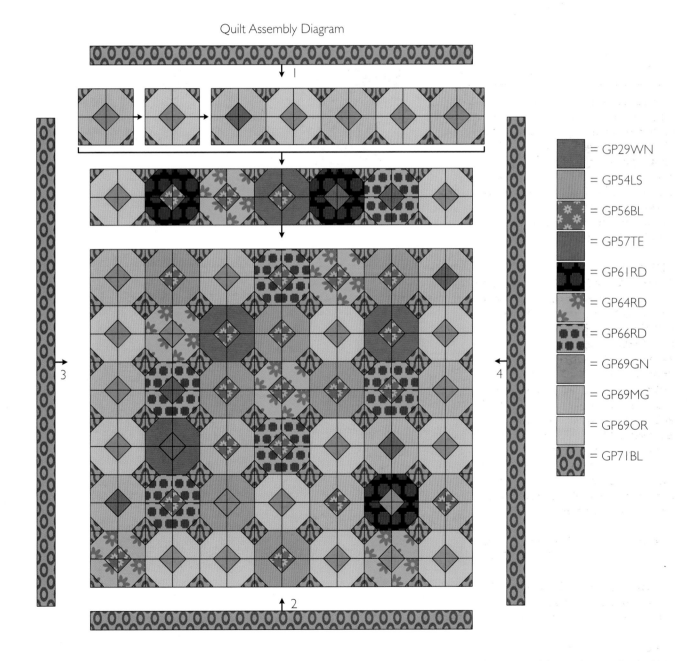

= GP29WN
= GP54LS
= GP56BL
= GP57TE
= GP61RD
= GP64RD
= GP66RD
= GP69GN
= GP69MG
= GP69OR
= GP71BL

Double Pinwheels Quilt ★★

LIZA PRIOR LUCY

My friend is a collector of antique quilts and has an incredible memory for unusual old quilt layouts. She sketched an interesting quilt for me that had small Pinwheels used as sashing around larger Pinwheels. I was intrigued. Here is my version in the deep colours on autumn flowers.

SIZE OF QUILT
The finished quilt will measure approx. 84in x 84in (213.5cm x 213.5cm).

MATERIALS
We have drawn the quilt showing the exact placement Liza used, however this is meant to be a 'scrappy style' quilt and exact placement of fabrics are not important. The only exception to this are the chartreuse and coal SHOT COTTON fabrics (SC12 and SC63) which are used in the small blocks and should be placed as shown.
Patchwork and Border Fabrics:

LOTUS LEAF
Umber   GP29UM: ¾yd (70cm)

Wine   GP29WN: ½yd (45cm)
CLOISONNE
Black   GP46BK: ¾yd (70cm)
Magenta   GP46MG: ½yd (45cm)
Teal   GP46TE: ½yd (45cm)
FLOWER BASKET
Black   GP48BK: ½yd (45cm)
Magenta   GP48MG: ½yd (45cm)

Rust	GP48RU: ½yd (45cm)
PAISLEY JUNGLE	
Purple	GP60PU: 2⅛yds (1.95m)
BEKAH	
Magenta	GP69MG: ½yd (45cm)
SPOT	
Magenta	GP70MG: ⅜yd (35cm)
Red	GP70RD: ⅜yd (35cm)
SHOT COTTON	
Persimmon	SC07: ¼yd (25cm)
Bittersweet	SC10: ¼yd (25cm)
Chartreuse	SC12: 2yds (1.85m)
Cobalt	SC45: ¼yd (25cm)
Aegean	SC46: ⅜yd (35cm)
Grape	SC47: ⅜yd (35cm)
Coal	SC63: ⅝yd (60cm)

Backing Fabric: 6¼yds (5.75m)
We suggest these fabrics for backing:
BROCADE FLORAL Crimson, GP68CR
LOTUS LEAF Umber, GP29UM

Binding:
SHOT COTTON
Grape   SC47: ¾yd (70cm)

Batting:
90in x 90in (228.5cm x 228.5cm).

Quilting thread:
Toning machine quilting thread.

Templates:

PATCH SHAPES
This quilt is made using 2 sizes of 'Pinwheel' blocks. The large blocks (finish to 12in (30.5cm)) are made with a large triangle patch shape (Template G) and the small blocks (finish to 4in (10.25cm)) are made with a small triangle patch shape (Template P). The large blocks are set on point in diagonal rows with the small blocks used as sashing. The edges of the quilt centre are finished using large and small half–blocks and the corners with template G triangles. The quilt centre is surrounded with a border which has corner posts pieced from small 'pinwheel' blocks.

CUTTING OUT
Template G: Cut 6⅞in (17.5cm) wide strips across the width of the fabric. Each strip will give you 10 patches per width. Cut 24 in GP29UM, GP46BK, 16 in GP29WN, GP46MG, GP69MG, 12 in GP46TE, GP48BK, GP48MG and GP48RU.
Template P: Cut 2⅞in (7.25cm) wide strips across the width of the fabric. Each strip will give you 26 patches per width. Cut 568 in SC12, 136 in SC63, 72 in GP70MG, GP70RD, SC47, 60 in SC46, 52 in SC07, SC10 and SC45.
Borders: From the length of the fabric cut 4 borders 69in x 8½in (175.25cm x 21.5cm) in GP69PU. These are a little oversized and will be trimmed to fit exactly later.

Binding: Cut 9 strips 2½in (6.5cm) wide across the width of the fabric in SC47.

Backing: Cut 2 pieces 40in x 90in (101.5cm x 228.5cm), 2 pieces 40in x 11in (101.5 x 28cm) and 1 piece 11in x 11in (28cm x 28cm) in backing fabric.

MAKING THE BLOCKS
Use a ¼in (6mm) seam allowance throughout. Using the quilt assembly as a guide to fabric placement piece a total of 13 large 'Pinwheel' blocks using the template G triangles and following block assembly diagrams a and b. The finished block can be seen in diagram c. Also piece 8 half–blocks for the quilt edges as shown in diagrams d and e. Piece the remaining template G triangles for the corners of the quilt centre as shown in the quilt assembly diagram.

The small 'Pinwheel blocks are pieced in the same way, this time using the template P triangles. Shot Cotton chartreuse (SC12) is used in all the blocks. Make the following numbers of blocks in the following fabric combinations: 28 in SC63/SC12, 18 in GP70MG/SC12, GP70RD/SC12, SC47/SC12, 15 in SC46/SC12, 13 in SC10/SC12 and SC45/SC12. Also piece 12 half–blocks in SC63/SC12.

MAKING THE QUILT
Lay out all the blocks as shown in the quilt assembly diagram. Note that the SC63/SC12 small 'Pinwheel' blocks and half–blocks are used at the intersections and edges of the diagonal rows. Separate the rows diagonally and join. Join the rows as shown in the quilt assembly diagram to form the quilt centre. Trim all the borders to fit exactly. Join the

Block Assembly Diagrams

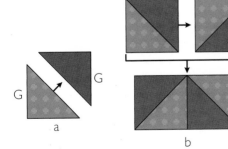

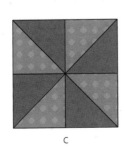

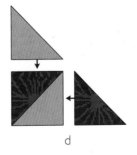

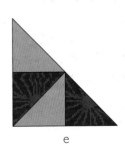

side borders to the quilt centre. Piece the remaining 16 small 'Pinwheel' blocks into 4 corner posts and add one to each end of the top and bottom borders then join to the quilt as shown in the quilt assembly diagram.

FINISHING THE QUILT
Press the quilt top. Seam the backing pieces using a ¼in (6mm) seam allowance to form a piece approx. 90in × 90in (228.5cm × 228.5cm). Layer the quilt top, batting and backing and baste together (see page 138). Using toning machine quilting thread, meander quilt loosely across the surface of the quilt. Trim the quilt edges and attach the binding (see page 139).

Quilt Assembly Diagram

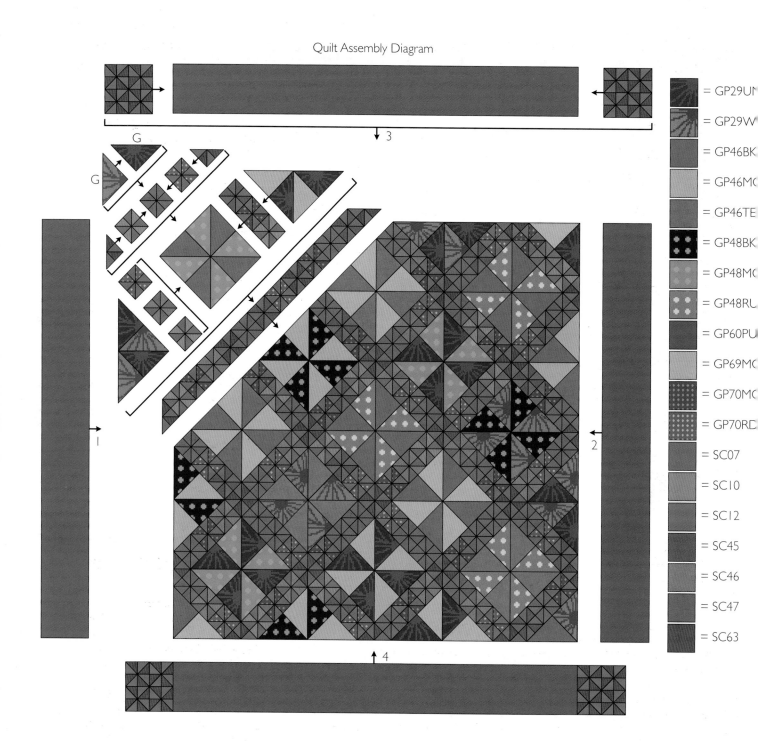

= GP29UN
= GP29W
= GP46BK
= GP46MC
= GP46TE
= GP48BK
= GP48MC
= GP48RU
= GP60PU
= GP69MC
= GP70MC
= GP70RD
= SC07
= SC10
= SC12
= SC45
= SC46
= SC47
= SC63

Economy Blue Patch Quilt ★★

LIZA PRIOR LUCY

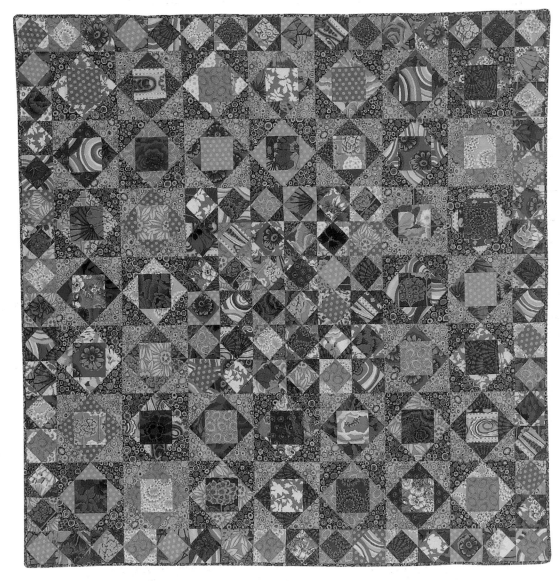

I have always loved every form of the diamond in a square block. The larger block in this quilt is called 'Economy Patch'. There is very little fabric left over after making this scrappy version. It is good economy!

SIZE OF QUILT
The finished quilt will measure approx. 64in x 64in (162.5cm x 162.5cm).

MATERIALS
This fabric list is a guide, don't worry about substituting other fabrics in if some are not available. We have drawn the quilt showing the exact placement Liza used, however this is meant to be a 'scrappy style' quilt and exact numbers and placement of fabric are not important. The only exception to this are the PAPERWEIGHT cobalt and sludge fabrics (GP20CB and GP20SL) which are used in the large blocks and should be placed as shown.

Buy ⅞yd (80cm) of each of the following fabrics.
PAPERWEIGHT Cobalt	GP20CB
PAPERWEIGHT Sludge	GP20SL

Buy ¼yd (25cm) of each of the following fabrics.

Light Patchwork Fabrics:
FLOATING FLOWERS Pastel	GP56PT
VERBENA Powder Blue	GP61PB
MINTON Blue	GP63BL
POTENTILLA Blue	GP64BL
JUNGLE STRIPE Blue	GP65BL
TARGETS Blue	GP67BL
BEKAH Blue	GP69BL

SPOT Duck Egg	GP70DE
ABORIGINAL DOTS Blue	GP71BL
SILHOUETTE ROSE Blue	GP77BL

Dark Patchwork Fabrics:
LOTUS LEAF Blue	GP29BL
ZINNIA Blue	GP31BL
KIMONO Cobalt/Turquoise	GP33CT
FLOWER BASKET Cobalt	GP48CB
FLOATING FLOWERS Blue	GP56BL
PAPER FANS Teal	GP57TE
VERBENA Cobalt	GP61CB
BEKAH Cobalt	GP69CB
SPOT Periwinkle	GP70PE
ABORIGINAL DOTS Delft	GP71DF

Backing Fabric: 4¼yds (3.9m)
We suggest these fabrics for backing:
ABORIGINAL DOTS Blue, GP71BL
MINTON Blue, GP63BL
POTENTILLA Blue, GP64BL

Binding:
PAPERWEIGHT
Cobalt   GP20CB: ⅝yd (60cm)

Batting:
72in × 72in (183cm × 183cm).

Quilting thread:
Pale blue machine quilting thread.

Templates:

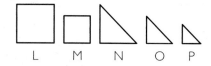

L M N O P

PATCH SHAPES

This quilt is made using 2 blocks. The small block is a diamond in a square block (finishes to 4in (10.25cm) which uses 1 square patch shape (Template M) and 1 triangle patch shape (Template P). The large block is the 'Economy Patch' block (finishes to 8in (20.25cm) which uses 1 square patch shape (Template L) and 2 triangle patch shapes (Templates O and N). Small blocks are pieced to form a centre section, then surrounded with large blocks, and finished with a border of small blocks.

CUTTING OUT

We recommend cutting as you go for this quilt. Several patch shapes are cut from each ¼yd (25cm) of fabric, it is not economical to use our usual 'strip cutting' method.
Template L: These are 4½in (11.5cm) squares.

Cut 20 in light fabrics and 20 in dark fabrics.
Template M: These are 3⅜in (8.5cm) squares. Cut 48 in light fabrics and 48 in dark fabrics.
Template P: These are 2⅞in (7.25cm) squares cut diagonally to form 2 triangles. Cut in sets of 4 matching triangles for each block. Cut a total of 192 (48 sets of 4) triangles in light fabrics and 192 (48 sets of 4) triangles in dark fabrics.
Template O: These are 3⅝in (9.25cm) squares cut diagonally to form 2 triangles. Cut in sets of 4 matching triangles for each block. Cut a total of 80 (20 sets of 4) triangles in light fabrics and 80 (20 sets of 4) triangles in dark fabrics.
Template N: These are 4⅞in (12.5cm) squares, cut diagonally to form 2 triangles. Cut in sets of 4 matching triangles for each block. Cut 80 (20 sets of 4) in GP20CB and 80 (20 sets of 4) in GP20SL.

Binding: Cut 7 strips 2½in (6.5cm) wide across the width of the fabric in GP20CB.

Backing: Cut 1 piece 40in × 72in (101.5cm × 183cm) and 1 piece 33in × 72in (84cm × 183cm) backing fabric.

MAKING THE BLOCKS
Use a ¼in (6mm) seam allowance

throughout. When piecing both the large and small blocks make lining up the triangles to the sides of the centre squares easy by folding the square in half and finger pressing a crease at the centre of each side, do the same on the triangles by creasing the centre of the long side. To position the triangle against the side line up the creases and pin at the centre spot. Feed carefully through the sewing machine to avoid stretching the bias edge of the triangle, add triangles to 2 opposite sides, then the other 2 opposite sides.

Following the small block assembly diagrams a, b and c piece 48 small blocks with dark fabric centres and light fabric triangles, and 48 small blocks with light fabric centres and dark fabric triangles, making a total of 96 small blocks.

Following the large block assembly diagrams d, e, f and g piece 20 large blocks with dark fabric centres, light fabric middle triangles and GP20CB outer triangles. Then make 20 with light fabric centres, dark fabric middle triangles and GP20SL outer triangles, making a total of 40 large blocks.

MAKING THE QUILT
Lay out all the blocks as shown in the quilt

Small Block Assembly Diagrams

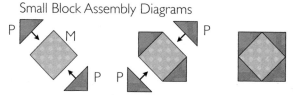

a   b   c

Large Block Assembly Diagrams

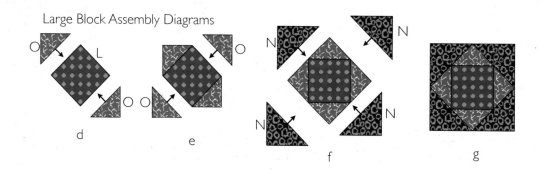

d   e   f   g

assembly diagram alternating the dark and light centres as shown. Piece the centre section by making 6 rows of 6 small blocks, piece the rows to form the quilt centre. Next piece the large blocks as shown and join to the centre. Lastly make 2 strips of 14 small blocks and add to the quilt sides, then make 2 strips of 16 small blocks and add to

the quilt top and bottom.

FINISHING THE QUILT
Press the quilt top. Seam the backing pieces using a ¼in (6mm) seam allowance to form a piece approx. 72in × 72in (183cm × 183cm). Layer the quilt top, batting and backing and baste together (see page 138). Using pale

blue machine quilting thread, stitch in the ditch in the seam lines. Then stipple quilt in the GP20SL triangles. Also in the 'light fabric' centre large blocks meander quilt following the shapes of the fabric designs. In the outer border, quilt in the centres of alternate blocks. Trim the quilt edges and attach the binding (see page 139).

Quilt Assembly Diagram

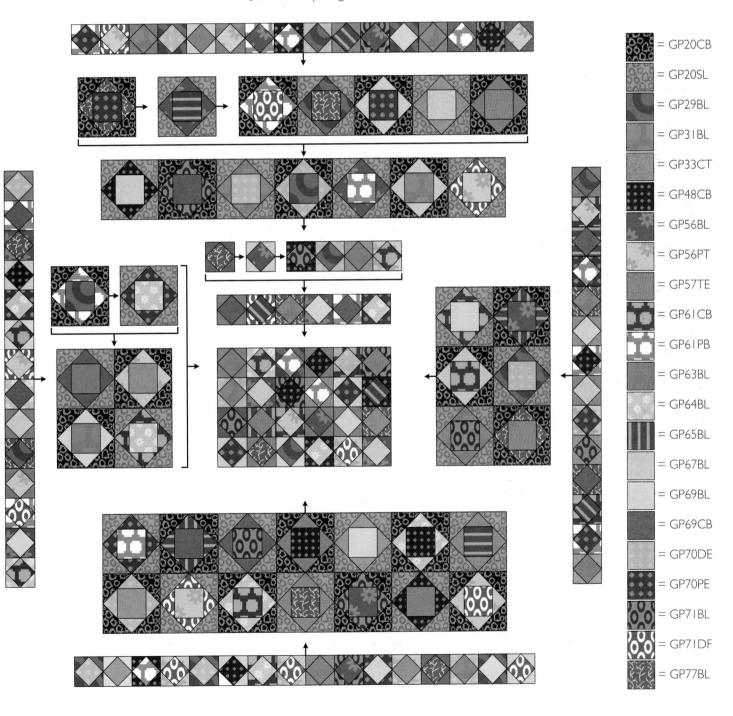

= GP20CB
= GP20SL
= GP29BL
= GP31BL
= GP33CT
= GP48CB
= GP56BL
= GP56PT
= GP57TE
= GP61CB
= GP61PB
= GP63BL
= GP64BL
= GP65BL
= GP67BL
= GP69BL
= GP69CB
= GP70DE
= GP70PE
= GP71BL
= GP71DF
= GP77BL

Paisley Stars Quilt ★★★

KAFFE FASSETT

When I designed the Jungle Stripe print I thought I'd use it in box shapes but I love the way it appears in these large stars. I used the deepest Aboriginal Dots to create a dark sky for my Paisley Stars. I'm particularly thrilled how the framed squares border turned out especially as I decided on the border after the quilt centre was worked out. Pauline had to fiddle to make it work and because it doesn't fit exactly you need a relaxed frame of mind when making this quilt.

SIZE OF QUILT
The finished quilt will measure approx. 70½in x 83in (179cm x 211cm).

MATERIALS
Patchwork and Border Fabrics:
FLOATING FLOWERS
Green   GP56GN: ⅜yd (35cm)
GUINEA FLOWER
Brown   GP59BR: ⅜yd (35cm)
JUNGLE STRIPE
Autumn   GP65AT: 1¼yds (1.15m)

Dark   GP65DK: 1¾yds (1.6m)
Green   GP65GN: 1½yds (1.4m)
Red   GP65RD: 1¼yds (1.15m)
PINKING FLOWER
Blue   GP66BL: ⅜yd (35cm)
SPOT
Magenta   GP70MG: ⅜yd (35cm)
ABORIGINAL DOTS
Chocolate   GP71CL: 2¼yds (2m)
Olive   GP71OV: 1yd (90cm)
SHOT COTTON
Bordeaux   SC54: ½yd (45cm)

Backing Fabric: 5½yds (5m)
Any of the JUNGLE STRIPE fabrics used in the quilt would be suitable for backing.

Binding:
SPOT
Magenta   GP70MG: ¾yd (70cm)

Batting:
79in x 91in (200.5cm x 231cm).

Quilting thread:
Toning machine quilting thread.

Templates:

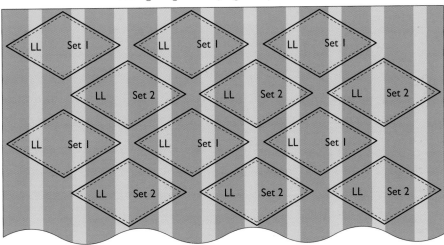

LL   MM   NN   OO

PP QQ   RR   SS   TT UU VV

PATCH SHAPES

Star blocks pieced from a diamond patch shape (Template LL) are pieced into a dark background of more diamonds. The edges and corners of the quilt centre are filled in using 3 triangle patch shapes (templates MM, NN and OO). The quilt centre is surrounded by a pieced border, with square blocks made using 1 square patch shape (Template PP) and 1 rectangle patch shape (Template QQ). These are set on point using a lozenge patch shape (Template RR) and a triangle patch shape (Template SS). The border also has pieced corner posts, made from 1 square patch shape (Template TT) and 2 rectangle patch shapes (Templates UU and VV).

CUTTING OUT

Cut the fabric in the order stated to prevent waste, use leftover strips for later templates trimming as appropriate.

Jungle Stripe Fabrics ONLY: Make transparent plastic templates for Templates LL, MM and NN as these are fussy cut. The stripes run down the length of the fabric. We have marked the templates with the stripe direction.

Template LL: Refer to the cutting diagram for Jungle Stripe fabrics. 3 identical diamonds can be cut across the width of the fabric, so 2 rows are required for each complete star (6 diamonds per set, pin each set together as you cut). The diagram shows how to cut 2 complete sets so that the patterns will repeat correctly. Note: Do not cut across the width of the fabric after each pair of sets, mark out all of the diamonds required in each fabric before cutting. Cut 32 (5 complete sets and

Cutting Diagram for Jungle Stripe Fabrics

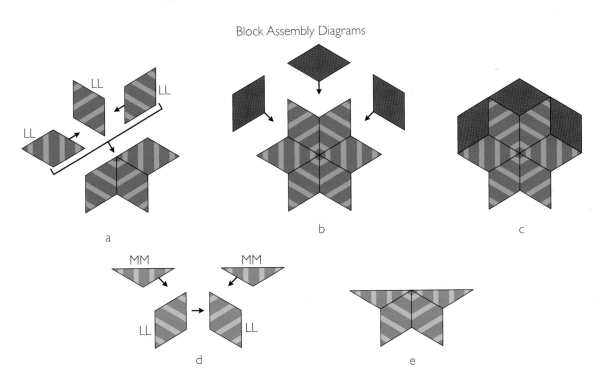

Block Assembly Diagrams

a

b

c

d

e

2 extra diamonds for a half block) in GP65DK, 28 (4 complete sets and 4 extra diamonds for 2 half blocks) in GP65GN, 24 (4 complete sets) in GP65AT and 20 (3 complete sets and 2 extra diamonds for a half block) in GP65RD. Reserve the remaining fabric for templates MM and NN.
Template MM: Cut these triangles so that they will match the extra template LL diamonds cut for half blocks. Cut 4 in GP65GN, 2 in GP65DK and GP65RD.
Template NN: Cut 3 in GP65DK, GP65GN and 2 in GP65RD.
All Other Fabrics:
Template LL: Cut 5¼in (13.5cm) strips across the width of the fabric. Each strip will give you 6 patches per width. Cut 61 in GP71CL.
Template MM: Cut 4 in GP71CL.
Template OO: Cut 2 in GP71CL.
Template TT: Cut 2⅞in (7.25cm) strips across the width of the fabric. Cut 4 in GP66BL.
Template QQ: 1½in (3.75cm) strips across the width of fabric. Each strip will give you 11 patches per width. Cut 32 in GP56GN, GP59BR, GP70MG and 28 in GP66BL.
Template PP: Cut 1½in (3.75cm) strips across the width of the fabric. Each strip will give you 26 patches per width. Cut 32 in GP56GN, GP59BR, GP70MG and 28 in GP66BL.
Template RR: Cut strips a little over 1½in (3.75) across the width of the fabric (use the template as a guide). Each strip will give you 9 patches per width. Cut 132 in GP71OV.
Template SS: Cut strips a little over 1¾in (4.5cm) across the width of the fabric (use the template as a guide). Each strip will give you 9 patches per width. Cut 132 in SC54.
Template VV: Cut 1½in (3.75cm) strips across the width of the fabric. Each strip will give you 8 patches per width. Cut 8 in

GP71OV.
Template UU: Cut 1½in (3.75cm) strips across the width of the fabric. Cut 8 in GP71OV.

Binding: Cut 8 strips 2½in (6.5cm) wide across the width of the fabric in GP70MG.

Backing: Cut 2 pieces 40in x 91in (101.5cm x 231cm) in backing fabric.

MAKING THE STAR BLOCKS
Use a ¼in (6mm) seam allowance throughout. Each full star block is made using a set of 6 identical template LL diamonds. Lay each set out and vary the look by rotating each diamond in turn, each set can be joined in 2 ways. Look at the photograph for help with this. Join the diamonds as shown in block assembly diagram a. There are variations to the full block at the edges of the quilt centre, so look carefully at the quilt assembly diagram before adding background diamonds. Add background diamonds to the blocks as shown in diagram b, using the inset seam method as shown in the Patchwork Knowhow section at the back of the book. A full block is shown in diagram c. Half blocks are pieced in a similar way, each using 2 template LL diamonds and 2 template MM triangles, as shown in diagrams d and e.

MAKING THE QUILT CENTRE
Lay out the blocks as shown in the quilt assembly diagram. Add filler triangles (templates MM and NN) and diamonds (template LL) to the edge blocks as shown in the quilt assembly diagram. The piecing sequence is marked on the quilt assembly diagram. This sequence has been carefully worked out so there are no nasty deep 'V' shaped inset seams to piece. Start by joining the first vertical column of blocks, stages 1–4.

Then move to the next column, adding a half block at the top, then slotting in the next block and so on, stages 5–9. Complete the quilt centre by following the whole sequence.

MAKING THE BORDER
These borders probably will not fit exactly, and as Kaffe comments, a relaxed attitude is a bonus! You may need to trim or extend the borders slightly to fit. First piece a total of 62 blocks as shown in border assembly diagram f. Then piece the inset triangles as shown in diagrams h and i. Set your seam allowance to a little less than ¼in (6mm). This will mean that the border will be a little larger than if stitched with the usual allowance. Piece the borders as shown in diagram j. Make 2 borders with 14 blocks set on point for the quilt top and bottom and 2 with 17 blocks for the quilt sides. Piece the corner posts using the same technique as for the border blocks but using a template TT square and 2 each of template UU and VV for each post. Adjust the lengths of the borders if necessary. Join the side borders to the quilt centre. Add a corner post to each end of the top and bottom borders and join to the quilt centre as shown in the quilt assembly diagram.

FINISHING THE QUILT
Press the quilt top. Seam the backing pieces using a ¼in (6mm) seam allowance to form a piece approx. 79in x 91in (200.5cm x 231cm). Layer the quilt top, batting and backing and baste together (see page 138). Using toning machine quilting thread, quilt in the ditch around the centre stars and border blocks. Also quilt lines across each star opposite to the fabric stripe direction, finally loosely stipple quilt in the GP71CL background diamonds. Trim the quilt edges and attach the binding (see page 139).

Border Assembly Diagrams

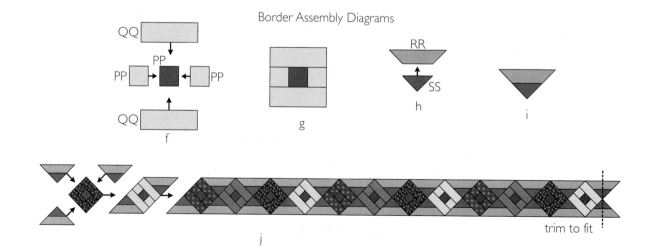

Quilt Assembly Diagram

= GP56GN   = GP65GN   = GP71CL

= GP59BR   = GP65RD   = GP71OV

= GP65AT   = GP66BL   = SC54

= GP65DK   = GP70MG

Spider Web Quilt ★★★

Kaffe Fassett

Inspired by a Grandmother's garden quilt in the same layout I thought a Spider Web would be far easier to make. I used the same palette of deep browns and ochres but dropped in higher reds and pinks. The black sashing gives the quilt a serious drama which could be transformed by a lighter sashing.

SIZE OF QUILT
The finished quilt will measure approx.
84¾in x 86½in (215cm x 220cm).

MATERIALS
Patchwork Fabrics:
ROMAN GLASS
Byzantine   GP01BY: ⅜yd (35cm)
PAPERWEIGHT
Algae   GP20AL: ⅜yd (35cm)
Gypsy   GP20GY: ½yd (45cm)
PAPER FANS
Ochre   GP57OC: ⅝yd (60cm)
Red   GP57RD: ¾yd (70cm)
GUINEA FLOWER
Brown   GP59BR: ⅝yd (60cm)

Yellow   GP59YE: ⅜yd (35cm)
PINKING FLOWER
Earth   GP66ER: ⅝yd (60cm)
Red   GP66RD: ¾yd (70cm)
SPOT
Burgundy   GP70BG: ½yd (45cm)
Magenta   GP70MG: ⅝yd (60cm)
Red   GP70RD: ⅝yd (60cm)
Taupe   GP70TA: ⅝yd (60cm)
ABORIGINAL DOTS
Delft   GP71DF: ¾yd (70cm)
Olive   GP71OV: ⅜yd (35cm)
Red   GP71RD: ⅜yd (35cm)
Rose   GP71RO: ⅞yd (80cm)
Rust   GP71RU: ¼yd (25cm)

SHOT COTTON
Coal   SC63: 1⅜yds (1.25m)

Border Fabric:
TARGETS
Red   GP67RD: 2⅝yds (2.4m)

Backing Fabric: 7yds (6.4m)
We suggest these fabrics for backing:
PAPERWEIGHT Gypsy, GP20GY
PINKING FLOWER Earth, GP66ER
SPOT Burgundy, GP70BG

Binding:
SPOT
Magenta   GP70MG: ¾yd (70cm)

Batting:
93in x 95in (236cm x 241cm).

Quilting thread:
Hand quilting thread in dark terracotta
Perlé embroidery thread in black.

Templates:

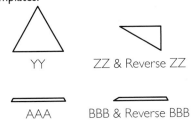

PATCH SHAPES
Strip sets of 5 different fabrics are joined and then cut to an equilateral triangle shape (Template YY). The triangles each have a dark sashing strip added to the base (Template AAA) and are then pieced into hexagonal blocks. 2 identical strip sets are needed to make 2 different blocks, (see block assembly diagram d). The hexagonal blocks are joined to form the quilt centre along with half blocks to fill in along the quilt sides. An additional triangle patch shape (Template ZZ & Reverse ZZ) is cut from the leftover strip sets, with another sashing strip (Template BBB & Reverse BBB) added to each triangle. These fill in the top and bottom edges of the quilt. The quilt centre is then surrounded with a simple border to complete the quilt.

CUTTING OUT
Strip Set Fabric for Templates YY and ZZ:
Cut 2in (5cm) strips across the width of the fabric. Cut 13 in GP71RO, 11 in GP57RD, GP71DF, 10 in GP66RD, 9 in GP59BR, GP66ER, GP70RD, GP70TA, 8 in GP57OC, GP70MG, 7 in GP20GY, GP70BG, 5 in GP01BY, GP71OV, 4 in GP20AL, GP59YE, GP71RD, 2 in GP71RU.

Template AAA: Cut 1in (2.5cm) strips across the width of the fabric. Each strip will give you 4 patches per width. Cut 135 in SC63.

Template BBB & Reverse BBB: Cut 1in (2.5cm) strips across the width of the fabric. Each strip will give you 4 patches per width. Cut 9 in SC63. Reverse the template by flipping it over, cut 9 Reverse BBB in SC63.

Borders: From the length of the fabric cut 2 borders 86in x 8in (218.5cm x 20.5cm) for the quilt top and bottom and 2 borders 73in x 8in (185.5cm x 20.5cm) for the quilt sides in GP67RD. These are a little oversized and will be trimmed to fit exactly later.

Binding: Cut 9 strips 2½in (6.5cm) wide across the width of the fabric in GP70MG.

Backing: Cut 2 pieces 40in x 93in (101.5cm x 236cm), 2 pieces 40in x 16in (101.5cm x 40.5cm) and 1 piece 14in x 16in (35.5cm x 40.5cm) in backing fabric.

MAKING THE BLOCKS
Use a ¼in (6mm) seam allowance throughout. First sort all the fabric strips into sets. Each set has 5 strips, refer to the quilt assembly diagram for fabric combinations. You will need 2 identical strip sets to make 2 blocks, Block A and Block B, which look very different (see block assembly diagram d). For the half blocks which fill the quilt sides only 1 strip set is needed.

Join the first strip set as shown in the cutting diagram for template YY, press carefully. Using template YY as shown cut the strip set cut into equilateral triangles. You will get 3 'A' triangles and 3 'B' triangles from each strip set. There will be a section uncut, reserve this for cutting the template ZZ & Reverse ZZ.

Take the 6 'A' triangles, join a template AAA sashing strip to each as shown in block assembly diagram a. Join to form Block A following diagrams b and c. Next take the 6 'B' triangles and 6 template AAA sashing strips and make a Block B in the same way. Make the strip sets, cut and piece one at a time to prevent the triangles being mixed up. Make a total of 20 blocks (10 Block A and 10 Block B). Also make 5 half blocks to fill the quilt sides.

Using the reserved strip set fabrics cut 9 template ZZ and 9 template Reverse ZZ as shown in the cutting diagram for template ZZ & Reverse ZZ. There are 8 matched pairs and 2 odd triangles. Join a template BBB or Reverse BBB sashing strip to each triangle as

Cutting Diagram for Template ZZ & Reverse ZZ

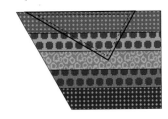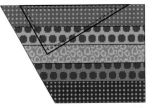

Cutting Diagram for Template YY

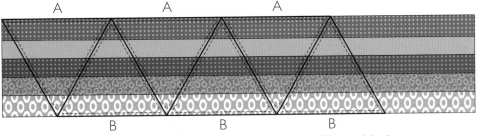

Make 2 identical strip sets to make 2 different blocks

appropriate. These make the filler triangles for the top and bottom of the quilt centre.

MAKING THE QUILT CENTRE

Lay out the blocks, half blocks and filler triangles as shown in the quilt assembly diagram. The piecing sequence is marked on the quilt assembly diagram. Using the inset seam method as shown in the Patchwork Knowhow section at the back of the book, start by joining the first vertical column of blocks, stages 1–6. Then move to the next column, adding the filler triangles to the top block first, stages 7–8, then joining it to the first column, stage 9. Slot in the next block and so on, stages 10–11. Complete the quilt centre by following the whole sequence.

ADDING THE BORDER

Trim the side borders to fit exactly and join to the quilt centre. Trim the top and bottom borders to fit exactly then join to the quilt centre as shown in the quilt assembly diagram.

FINISHING THE QUILT

Press the quilt top. Seam the backing pieces using a ¼in (6mm) seam allowance to form a piece approx. 93in x 95in (236cm x 241cm). Layer the quilt top, batting and backing and baste together (see page 138). Using dark terracotta hand quilting thread, quilt the centre as shown in the quilting diagram. The black dots at the block intersections show the position of French knots, embroider these in black perlé thread. Free motion quilt the border following the pattern in the fabric. Trim the quilt edges and attach the binding (see page 139).

Quilting Diagram

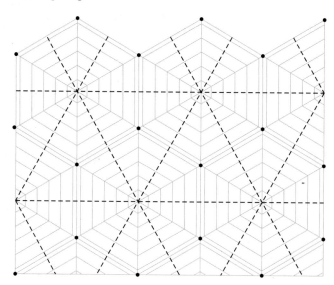

Block assembly diagrams

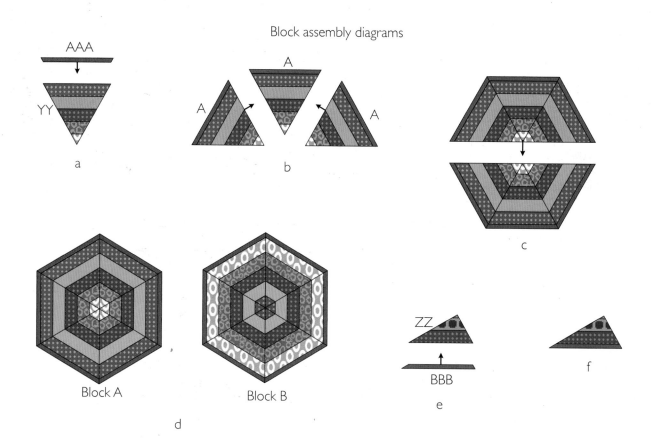

a

b

c

Block A

Block B

d

e

f

92

Quilt Assembly Diagram

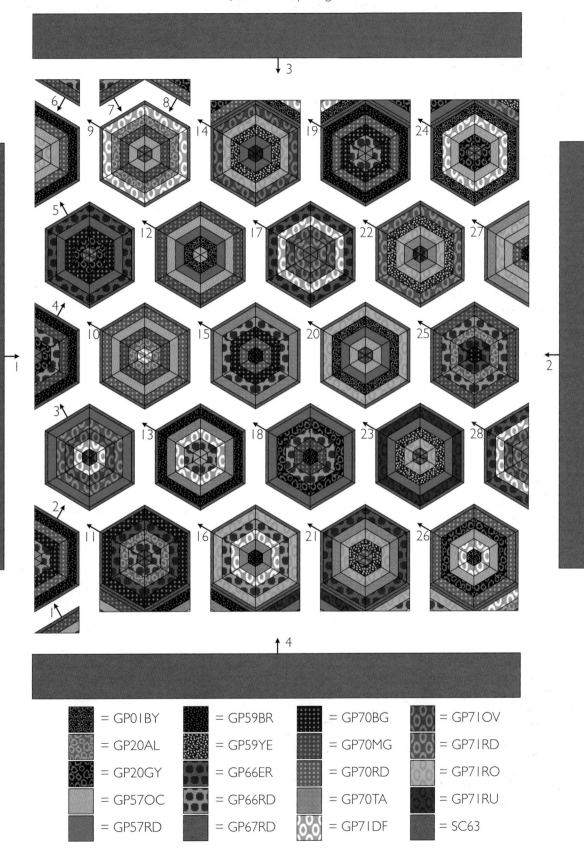

= GP01BY	= GP59BR	= GP70BG	= GP71OV
= GP20AL	= GP59YE	= GP70MG	= GP71RD
= GP20GY	= GP66ER	= GP70RD	= GP71RO
= GP57OC	= GP66RD	= GP70TA	= GP71RU
= GP57RD	= GP67RD	= GP71DF	= SC63

Chintz Quilt ★

KAFFE FASSETT

When I spotted a stunning English quilt (1810 - 1825) using English chintz prints I wasn't aware it was a snowball block for the longest time. Suddenly I realised the corners were similar prints as the snowball so virtually disappeared, yet there was a pleasing roundness and mirror imagery that kept you looking at the quilt. I used my dotty Guinea Flower in green to create the corners on the chintz like prints in our collection. There is a percentage of cream, yellow and pink in these leafy prints that make for a sunny, dappled feel. Philip Jacob's Lilac Rose print makes a delicious centre with its pistachio coloured border.

SIZE OF QUILT
The finished quilt will measure approx.
75½in x 90½in (192cm x 230cm).

MATERIALS
Patchwork and Border Fabrics:

LOTUS LEAF
Jade	GP29JA:	⅝yd (60cm)
Yellow	GP29YE:	⅜yd (35cm)

DAHLIA BLOOMS
Vintage	GP54VN:	⅝yd (60cm)

GUINEA FLOWER
Green	GP59GN:	2¼yds (2.1m)

PERSIMMON
Pink	GP74PK:	1½yds (1.4m)

SILHOUETTE ROSE
Duck Egg	GP77DE:	⅜yd (35cm)

GRANDIOSE
Natural	PJ13NL:	⅝yd (60cm)
Ochre	PJ13OC:	⅝yd (60cm)
Taupe	PJ13TA:	⅝yd (60cm)

TULIP
Gold	PJ14GD:	⅝yd (60cm)
Pink	PJ14PK:	⅝yd (60cm)
Yellow	PJ14YE:	⅝yd (60cm)

BLOUSEY
Natural	PJ15NL:	⅝yd (60cm)
Pink	PJ15PK:	⅝yd (60cm)

LILAC ROSE
Lilac	PJ17LI:	⅞yd (80cm)

Backing Fabric: 6½yds (6m)
We suggest these fabrics for backing:
LOTUS LEAF Jade, GP29JA
LILAC ROSE Lilac, PJ17LI

Binding:
SILHOUETTE ROSE
Duck Egg   GP77DE: ¾yd (70cm)

Batting:
84in × 99in (213cm × 251.5cm).

Quilting Thread:
Toning machine quilting thread.
Taupe hand quilting thread.

Templates:

WW   XX

PATCH SHAPES

The centre of this quilt is a panel cut to size, surrounded by 2 simple borders. This section is then surrounded with traditional Snowball blocks, made from an octagon and four triangles, in this case it is made 'the easy way' by using a large square (Template WW) and 4 small squares (Template XX) for each block. The small squares are placed over the corners of the large squares and stitched diagonally. They are then trimmed and flipped back to replace the corners of the large square. The centre is then surrounded with simple border to complete the quilt.

CUTTING OUT

Cut the fabric in the order stated to prevent waste.
Centre Panel: Cut 1 rectangle 17in × 24½in (43.25cm × 62.25cm) in PJ17LI.
Border 1: Cut 2 strips 24½in × 2½in (62.25cm × 6.25cm) for the sides and 2 strips 21in × 2½in (53.5cm × 6.25cm) for the top and bottom in GP77DE.
Border 2: Cut 2 strips 28½in × 1½in (72.5cm × 3.75cm) for the sides and 2 strips 23in × 1½in (58.5cm × 3.75cm) for the top and bottom in GP74PK.
Border 3: Cut 9 strips 4½in (11.5cm) wide across the width of fabric in GP74PK. Join as necessary and cut 2 strips 4½in × 83in (11.5cm × 211cm) for the sides of the quilt and 2 strips 4½in × 76in (11.5cm × 193cm) for the top and bottom of the quilt.
Template WW: Cut 8in (20.25cm) strips across the width of the fabric. Each strip will give you 5 patches per full width. Cut 10 in PJ15NL, 8 in GP29JA, GP54VN, PJ13NL,

PJ13OC, PJ13TA, PJ14GD, PJ15PK, 6 in PJ14PK, PJ14YE, 5 in GP29YE and 4 in PJ17LI.
Template XX: Cut 2¾in (7cm) strips across the width of the fabric. Each strip will give you 14 patches per width. Cut 348 in GP59GN.

Binding: Cut 9 strips 2½in (6.5cm) wide across the width of the fabric in GP77DE.

Backing: Cut 2 pieces 40in × 99in (101.5cm × 251.5cm), 2 pieces 40in × 5in (101.5cm × 12.75cm) and 1 piece 20in × 5in (50.75cm × 12.75cm) in backing fabric.

MAKING THE CENTRE PANEL

Use a ¼in (6mm) seam allowance throughout. Take the centre panel of PJ17LI fabric and join a Border 1 side to each side. Then join the Border 1 top and bottom to the top and bottom of the centre panel. Press carefully and join border 2 in the same way as shown in the quilt centre assembly diagram.

MAKING THE SNOWBALL BLOCKS

To make the Snowball blocks take one large square (template WW) and four small squares (template XX). Place one small square, right sides together onto each corner of the large square, matching the edges carefully as shown in block assembly diagram a. Stitch diagonally across the small squares as shown in diagram b. Trim the corners to a ¼in (6mm) seam allowance and press the corners out (diagram c). Make 87 blocks.

MAKING THE QUILT

Use a ¼in (6mm) seam allowance throughout. Lay out all the blocks as shown in the quilt assembly diagram. Piece the snowball blocks into sections as shown and join to the centre panel. Finally add border 3, first the sides, then the top and bottom as shown in the quilt assembly diagram.

Block Assembly Diagrams

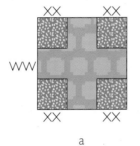
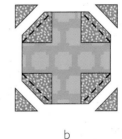
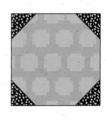

a   b   c

Quilt Centre Assembly Diagram

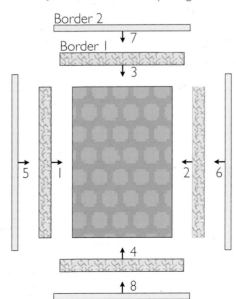

FINISHING THE QUILT

Press the quilt top. Seam the backing pieces using a ¼in (6mm) seam allowance to form a piece approx 84in × 99in (213cm × 251.5cm). Layer the quilt top, batting and backing and baste together (see page 138). Using toning machine quilting thread quilt in the ditch around the blocks and in the border seams, free motion quilt the centre panel following the flowers and foliage in the fabric print, quilt the outer border in the same way. On the centre of each snowball block hand quilt a 4¾in (12cm) diameter circle, using taupe thread. Trim the quilt edges and attach the binding (see page 139).

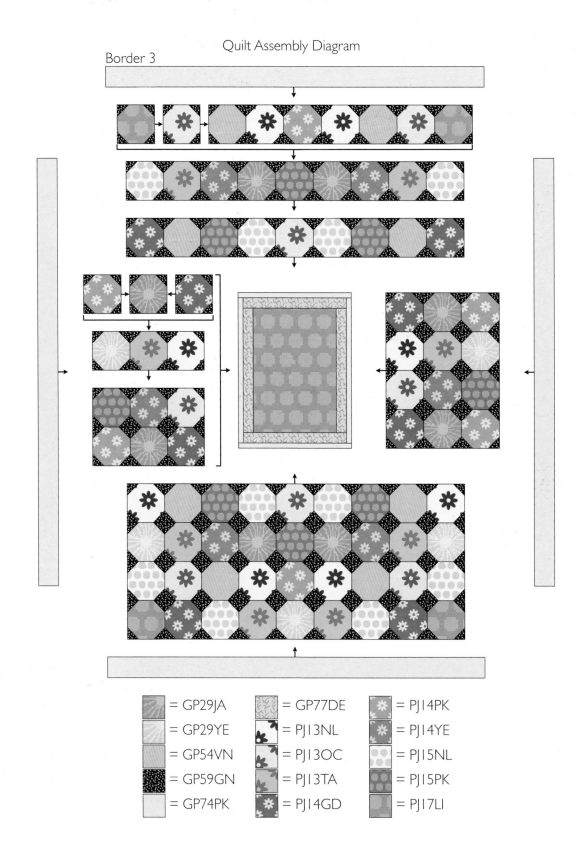

Quilt Assembly Diagram

Border 3

	= GP29JA		= GP77DE		= PJ14PK
	= GP29YE		= PJ13NL		= PJ14YE
	= GP54VN		= PJ13OC		= PJ15NL
	= GP59GN		= PJ13TA		= PJ15PK
	= GP74PK		= PJ14GD		= PJ17LI

Knot Garden Quilt ★ ★ ★

KAFFE FASSETT

I did this mostly in pinks in Caravan Of Quilts. The English bordered layout seemed worth a revisit. This version is softer pastels that look so elegant.

SIZE OF QUILT
The finished quilt will measure approx.
73in x 73in (185.5cm x 185.5cm).

MATERIALS
Patchwork Fabrics:
PAPERWEIGHT
Lime   GP20LM: ⅝yd (60cm)
KIMONO
Pink/Orange   GP33PO: 1yd (90cm)

FLOWER BASKET
Pink   GP48PK: ⅜yd (35cm)
DAHLIA BLOOMS
Spring   GP54SP: 1⅜yds (1.25m)
FLOATING FLOWERS
Pastel   GP56PT: ⅜yd (35cm)
PAPER FANS
Cream   GP57CM: ¼yd (25cm)
GUINEA FLOWER
Green   GP59GN: ⅛yd (15cm)

Mauve   GP59MV: ¼yd (25cm)
PAISLEY JUNGLE
Grey   GP60GY: ⅜yd (35cm)
PINKING FLOWER
Pink   GP66PK: ¼yd (25cm)
BROCADE FLORAL
Lavender   GP68LV: ¼yd (25cm)
Pink   GP68PK: ½yd (45cm)
SPOT
Duck Egg   GP70DE: 1½yds (1.4m)

Mint   GP70MT: ⅜yd (35cm)
Periwinkle   GP70PE: ⅝yd (60cm)
Turquoise   GP70TQ: ¼yd (25cm)
ABORIGINAL DOTS
Blue   GP71BL: ⅛yd (15cm)

Backing Fabric: 4¾yds (4.4m)
We suggest these fabrics for backing:
GUINEA FLOWER Mauve, GP59MV
PAISLEY JUNGLE Grey, GP60GY
DAHLIA BLOOMS Spring, GP54SP

Binding:
GUINEA FLOWER
Green   GP59GN: ¾yd (70cm)

Batting:
80in x 80in (203cm x 203cm).

Quilting thread:
Dark cream machine quilting thread.

Templates:

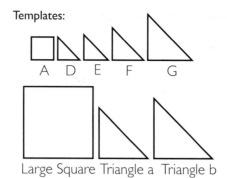

A D E F G

Large Square   Triangle a   Triangle b

PATCH SHAPES

This medallion style quilt is formed around a large central section with, 4 simple borders with corner posts and 2 pieced borders. The central square patch shape is cut to 10in (25.5cm), this is surrounded by triangles (Triangle a) cut to size. Then comes the first simple border with square corner posts (cut to size). This centre section is then set on

point with the addition of triangular sections pieced using 2 triangle patch shapes (Template E and Triangle b which is cut to size). The second simple border with square corner posts (cut to size) is then added. Next is a pieced border made with 1 square patch shape (Template A) and 1 triangle patch shape (Template D), the ends of this section are pieced slightly oversized and are trimmed to fit exactly, this border also has square corner posts (cut to size). This is followed by another simple border with square corner posts (cut to size). Another pieced border is next, made up of 1 square patch shape (Template A) pieced into 4 patch blocks and 2 triangle patch shapes (Templates F & G). The quilt is finished with a final simple border.

CUTTING OUT

To prevent waste please cut the fabric in the

Block Assembly Diagrams

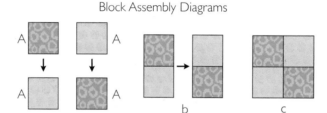

a   b   c

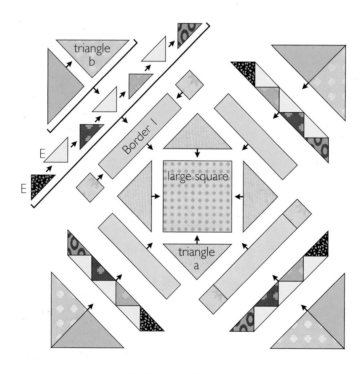

Quilt Assembly Diagram 1

order stated. Trim and use leftover strips for later templates as appropriate.

Border 1: Cut 4 strips 13¾in × 3¼in (35cm × 8.25cm) in GP68PK and 4 corner posts 3¼in (8.25cm) square in GP56PT.

Border 2: Cut 4 strips 27in × 4¼in (68.5cm × 10.75cm) in GP20LM and 4 corner posts 4¼in (10.75cm) square in GP68LV.

Border 3: Cut 4 corner posts 4¾in (12cm) square in GP56PT.

Border 4: Cut 5 strips 4½in (11.5cm) wide across the width of the fabric in GP33PO. Join as necessary and cut strips 43in × 4½in (109.25cm × 11.5cm). Also cut 4 corner posts 4½in (11.5cm) square in GP54SP.

Border 6: Cut 8 strips 3½in (9cm) wide across the width of the fabric in GP54SP. Join as necessary and cut 2 strips 68in × 3½in (173cm × 9cm) and 2 strips 74in × 3½in (188cm × 9cm).

Large Square: Fussy cut 1 × 10in (25.5cm) square in GP48PK, centring on a basket.

Triangle a: Cut 2 × 7⅝in (19.5cm) squares in GP60GY. Cut each square once diagonally to form 2 triangles. Total 4 triangles.

Triangle b: Cut 4 × 7⅞in (20cm) squares, 2 in GP33PO and 2 in GP70MT. Cut each square once diagonally to form 2 triangles. Total 8 triangles.

Template A: Cut 3½in (9cm) wide strips across the width of the fabric. Each strip will give you 11 patches per width. Cut 20 in GP66PK, 19 in GP68PK, 17 in GP54SP, 16 in GP57CM, GP70TQ, 15 in GP48PK, GP59MV, 12 in GP60GY, 10 in GP20LM and 4 in GP56PT.

Template E: Cut 3in (7.75cm) wide strips across the width of the fabric. Each strip will give you 12 patches per width. Place the template with the long side along the cut edge of the strip, this will ensure the long side of the triangles will not have a bias edge. Cut 12 in GP54SP, 4 in GP59GN, GP70PE, GP70TQ and GP71BL.

Template D: Cut 2¾in (7cm) wide strips across the width of the fabric. Each strip will give you 13 patches per width. Place the template with the long side along the cut edge of the strip, this will ensure the long side of the triangles will not have a bias edge. Cut 72 in GP70PE.

Template F: Cut 5⅛in (13cm) wide strips across the width of the fabric. Each strip will give you 14 patches per width. Cut 32 in GP70DE.

Template G: Cut 4⅞in (12.5cm) wide strips across the width of the fabric. Each strip will give you 7 patches per width. Place the template with the long side along the cut

edge of the strip, this will ensure the long side of the triangles will not have a bias edge. Cut 40 in GP70DE.

Binding: Cut 8 strips 2½in (6.25cm) wide across the width of the fabric GP59GN.

Backing: Cut 2 pieces 80in × 40in (203cm × 101.5cm) in backing fabric.

MAKING THE QUILT
Use a ¼in (6mm) seam allowance throughout and refer to the quilt assembly diagrams for fabric placement. Take the centre square and add the 4 'triangle a' shapes as shown in quilt assembly diagram 1. Add border 1 as shown. Sub–piece the next sections as shown and add to the centre.

Next add border 2 as shown in quilt assembly diagram 2. Sub–piece border 3 and trim to fit exactly, then add to the centre as shown. Once this section is complete, move

on to quilt assembly diagram 3.

Add border 4, then sub–piece border 5. Make a total of 28 four patch blocks following block assembly diagrams a and b, the finished block can be seen in diagram c. Piece the four patch blocks with the triangles (templates F and G) into borders and add to the quilt centre. Finally add border 6 to complete the quilt.

FINISHING THE QUILT
Press the quilt top. Seam the backing pieces using a ¼in (6mm) seam allowance to form a piece approx. 80in × 80in (203cm × 203cm). Layer the quilt top, batting and backing and baste together (see page 138). Using a dark cream machine quilting thread stitch–in–the–ditch along the seam lines. Also stipple quilt in the plain borders and in the large centre triangles. You can also follow the floral prints for added interest. For border 5 quilt lines offset by 1¼in (3.25cm) from the edges of the 4 patch blocks. Trim the quilt edges and attach the binding (see page 139).

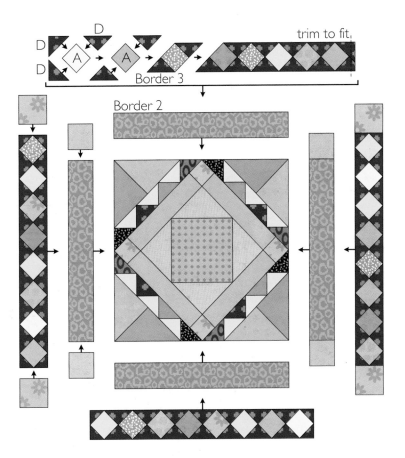

Quilt Assembly Diagram 2

Quilt Assembly Diagram 3

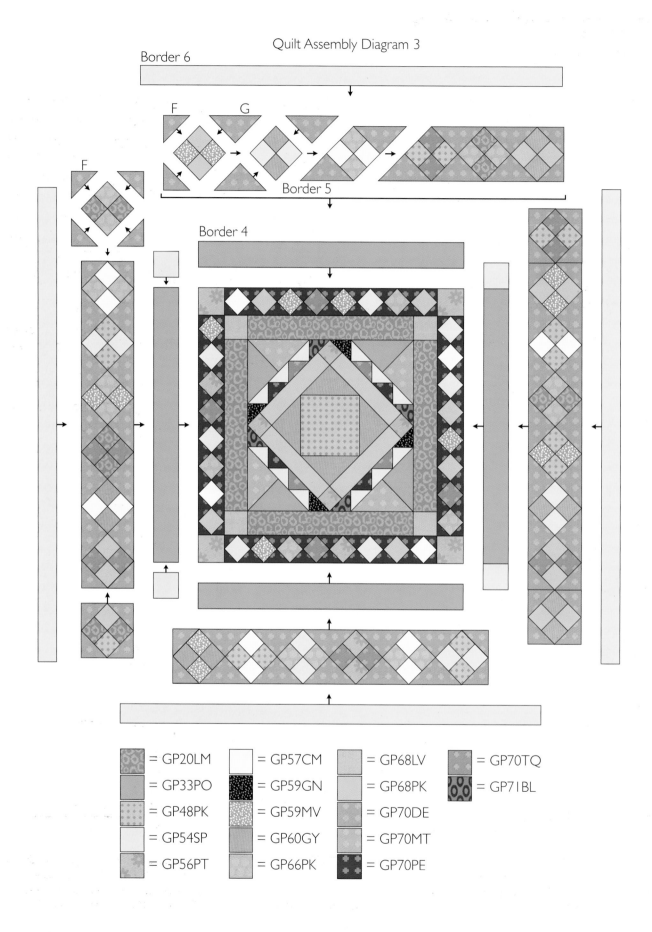

= GP20LM	= GP57CM	= GP68LV	= GP70TQ
= GP33PO	= GP59GN	= GP68PK	= GP71BL
= GP48PK	= GP59MV	= GP70DE	
= GP54SP	= GP60GY	= GP70MT	
= GP56PT	= GP66PK	= GP70PE	

Zig Zag Quilt ★★★

LIZA PRIOR LUCY

For maximum impact Liza fussy cut Kaffe's Jungle Stripe in the red and autumn colourways and punctuated them with Spot in hot shades. Kaffe thought it looked like those wonderful, whirling Mexican skirts. The red Targets border is the perfect finishing touch.

SIZE OF QUILT
The finished quilt will measure approx.
97in x 97in (246cm x 246cm).

MATERIALS
Patchwork Fabrics:
JUNGLE STRIPE
Autumn   GP65AT: 3yds (2.75m)
Red   GP65RD: 3yds (2.75m)
SPOT
Burgundy   GP70BG: ¾yd (70cm)
Fuchsia   GP70FU: 1yd (90cm)
Magenta   GP70MG: ¾yd (70cm)
Red   GP70RD: ¾yd (70cm)

Border Fabric:
TARGETS
Red   GP67RD: 3yds (2.75m)

Backing Fabric:
PINKING FLOWER
Red   GP66RD: 9⅜yds (8.6m)

Binding:
SPOT
Burgundy   GP70BG: ⅞yd (80cm)

Batting:
105in x 105in (266.5cm x 266.5cm).

Quilting thread:
Toning machine quilting thread.

Templates:

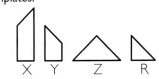

PATCH SHAPES
This quilt is pieced in columns, starting at the bottom with a triangle patch shape (Template Z). 2 lozenge patch shapes (Templates X and Y) are then added

alternately, to make a column. The columns are then joined and the top edge is filled using more template Z triangles and a further triangle patch shape (Template R). The quilt centre is surrounded with a simple border to complete the quilt.

SPECIAL CUTTING NOTES
The Jungle Stripe fabrics used in this quilt have 4 different stripe designs running along the length of the fabric. We have provided a cutting diagram as it is tricky to cut, cut all fabric right side up. DO NOT cut folded fabric as the angles in templates X and Y do not work in reverse. The jungle stripe fabric is cut in 3in (7.6cm) strips, working on one 23in (58.5cm) long panel at a time. When cutting don't be concerned with getting each section centred exactly. It will only be possible to get 12 strips (3 of each design) from each panel of fabric. This means you will need to waste about every 5th stripe. Be careful to cut equal amounts of each stripe design.

CUTTING OUT
Please read the Special Cutting Notes above before cutting any fabric. Cut the fabric in the order stated to prevent waste.
Templates X and Y: Cut panels 23in (58.5cm) by the width of the fabric. Cut 4 panels in GP65AT and GP65RD. Using the cutting diagram for Jungle Stripe fabrics as a guide cut 3in (7.6cm) wide strips down the length of the fabric as described in the Special Cutting Notes. Cut a total of 96 Template X (24 of each design) and 96 of Template Y (24 of each design) in GP65AT and GP65RD.
Cut 1 panel 23in (58.5cm) by the width of the fabric in GP70BG, GP70FU, GP70MG and GP70RD. Using the same technique as for the Jungle Stripe fabrics cut 3in (7.6cm) wide strips down the length of the fabric. Cut 12 strips in GP70BG, GP70FU, GP70RD and 6 strips in GP70MG. From these strips cut 24 of Template X and 24 of Template Y in GP70BG, GP70FU, GP70RD and 12 of Template X and 12 of Template Y in GP70MG. Reserve the remaining GP70MG panel for Template Z.
Template R: Cut a 4⅜in (11cm) strip across the width of the fabric. Cut 2 in GP70FU. Reserve the remaining fabric and trim for template Z.
Template Z: Cut 4⅛in (10.5cm) strips across the width of the fabric. Each strip will give you 8 patches per full width. Place the template with the long side along the cut

edge of the strip, this will ensure the long side of the triangles will not have a bias edge. Cut 12 in GP70MG and 11 in GP70FU.

Borders: From the length of the fabric cut 2 borders 98in × 6½in (249cm × 16.5cm) for the quilt top and bottom and 2 borders 86in × 6½in (218.5cm × 16.5cm) for the quilt sides in GP67RD. These are a little oversized and will be trimmed to fit exactly later.

Binding: Cut 10 strips 2½in (6.5cm) wide

across the width of the fabric in GP70BG.
Backing: Cut 2 pieces 40in × 105in (101.5cm × 266.5cm) and 1 piece 26in × 105in (66cm × 266.5cm) in GP66RD.

MAKING THE QUILT CENTRE
Sort the Jungle Stripe fabrics by the 8 design elements (4 from each colourway). The quilt centre is pieced in 12 columns, each with the same colour and design element in the same position. This means that when the columns are joined the zig zag pattern will repeat

Column Assembly Diagram

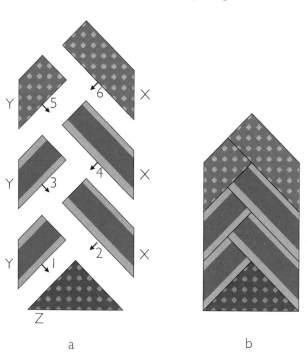

a   b

Cutting Diagram for Jungle Stripe Fabrics

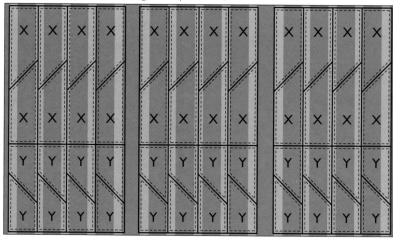

across the width of the quilt. Refer to the quilt assembly diagram and photograph for fabric position.

Using a ¼in (6mm) seam allowance throughout, piece each column from the bottom, starting with a template Z triangle. Follow column assembly diagrams a and b adding template Y and template X lozenges alternately. Make 12 columns and join carefully, the edges will be a bit stretchy as they are bias cut. Fill in the top edge with template Z triangles, using the inset seam method as shown in the Patchwork Knowhow section at the back of the book. Finally add the template R triangles to the top corners to complete the quilt centre.

ADDING THE BORDERS
Trim the side borders to fit the quilt sides exactly and join to the quilt centre. Trim the top and bottom borders to fit exactly then join to the quilt as shown in the quilt assembly diagram.

FINISHING THE QUILT
Press the quilt top. Seam the backing pieces using a ¼in (6mm) seam allowance to form a piece approx 105in × 105in (266.5cm × 266.5cm). Layer the quilt top, batting and backing and baste together (see page 138). Using toning machine quilting thread, meander quilt across the quilt centre. In the border meander quilt loosely following the circles in the fabric design. Trim the quilt edges and attach the binding (see page 139).

Quilt Assembly Diagram

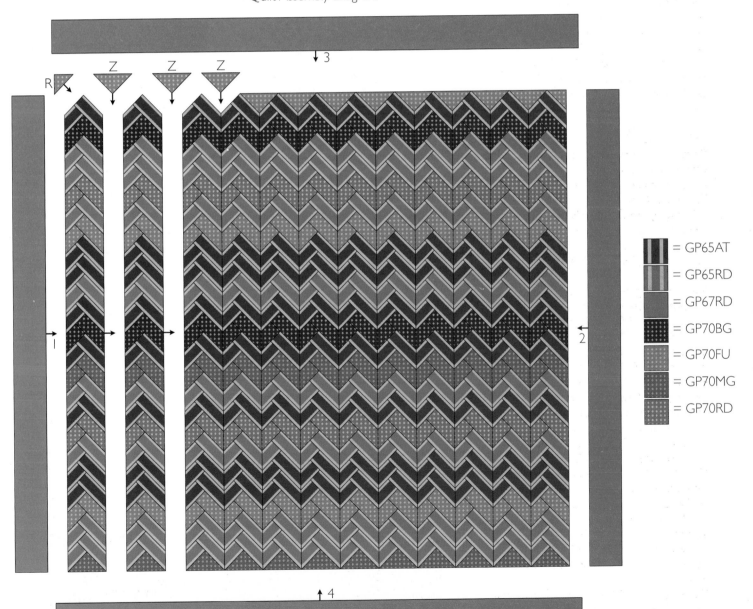

= GP65AT
= GP65RD
= GP67RD
= GP70BG
= GP70FU
= GP70MG
= GP70RD

Garden Rainbow Quilt ★

ROBERTA HORTON

Each year I aspire to a garden filled with a whole colour wheel's worth of blooms. Real flowers need sun or shade and require water or are drought tolerant. With Kaffe's fabrics I can make my garden grow just as I like with no snails or aphids.

SIZE OF QUILT
The finished quilt will measure approx. 82in x 76in (208cm x 193cm).

MATERIALS
Patchwork Fabrics:
PAPERWEIGHT

Algae	GP20AL:	¼yd (25cm)
Cobalt	GP20CB:	¼yd (25cm)
Lime	GP20LM:	¼yd (25cm)
Pumpkin	GP20PN:	¼yd (25cm)

FLOATING FLOWERS

Blue	GP56BL:	¼yd (25cm)
Yellow	GP56YE:	¼yd (25cm)

PAPER FANS

Green	GP57GN:	¼yd (25cm)

POTENTILLA

Green	GP64GN:	¼yd (25cm)
Red	GP64RD:	¼yd (25cm)

PINKING FLOWER

Gold	GP66GD:	¼yd (25cm)
Red	GP66RD:	¼yd (25cm)

BROCADE FLORAL

Crimson	GP68CR:	¼yd (25cm)

BEKAH

Green	GP69GN:	¼yd (25cm)
Plum	GP69PL:	¼yd (25cm)

ABORIGINAL DOTS

Lime	GP71LM:	¼yd (25cm)
Rose	GP71RO:	¼yd (25cm)

WOVEN HAZE STRIPE

Persimmon	HZS01:	½yd (45cm)

Mustard	HZS02:	½ yd (45cm)
Sunshine	HZS06:	½ yd (45cm)
Raspberry	HZS12:	½ yd (45cm)
Green	HZS16:	½ yd (45cm)
Lavender	HZS17:	½ yd (45cm)
Pine	HZS19:	½ yd (45cm)
Aegean	HZS20:	½ yd (45cm)

Border:
PAISLEY JUNGLE

Tangerine	GP60TN:	1⅜yds (1.3m)

Backing Fabric: 7⅜yds (6.75m)
We suggest these fabrics for backing:
MINTON Maroon, GP63MR
BEKAH Plum, GP69PL

Quilt Assembly Diagram

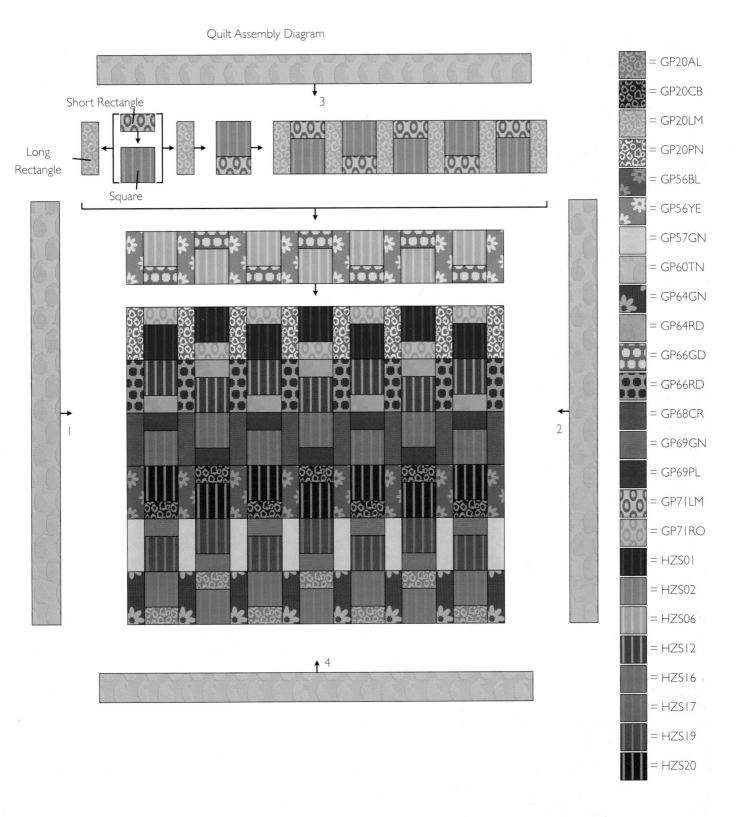

Long Rectangle

Short Rectangle

Square

1

2

3

4

= GP20AL
= GP20CB
= GP20LM
= GP20PN
= GP56BL
= GP56YE
= GP57GN
= GP60TN
= GP64GN
= GP64RD
= GP66GD
= GP66RD
= GP68CR
= GP69GN
= GP69PL
= GP71LM
= GP71RO
= HZS01
= HZS02
= HZS06
= HZS12
= HZS16
= HZS17
= HZS19
= HZS20

BROCADE FLORAL Crimson, GP68CR

Binding:
ROMAN GLASS
Gold   GP01GD: ¾yd (70cm)

Batting:
90in x 84in (228.5cm x 213.5cm).

Quilting thread:
Toning and variegated machine quilting threads.

PATCH SHAPES
This quilt is made using 1 square and 2
rectangle patch shapes, all are cut to size and no
templates are provided for these very simple
shapes. The patches are joined into rows by
colour and then pieced to form the quilt centre.
The quilt is finished with a simple border.

CUTTING OUT
Long Rectangle: Cut 3½in (9cm) strips
across the width of the fabric. Each strip will
give you 4 patches per width. From these cut
3½in x 9½in (9cm x 24.25cm) rectangles.
Cut 8 in GP20LM, GP20PN, GP56BL,
GP56YE, GP57GN, GP64GN, GP66RD and
GP68CR.
Short Rectangle: Cut 6½in (16.5cm) strips
across the width of the fabric. From these
cut 3½in x 6½in (9cm x 16.5cm) rectangles.
Cut 7 in GP20AL, GP20CB, GP64RD,
GP66GD, GP69GN, GP69PL, GP71LM and
GP71RO. Note for fabrics GP69GN and
GP69PL there is plenty of fabric to fussy cut
rectangles centring on the bold blooms. See
the photograph for details.
Square: Cut 6½in (16.5cm) strips across the
width of the fabric. Each strip will give you 6
patches per width. From these cut 6½in
(16.5cm) squares, cut 7 in HZS01, HZS02,
HZS06, HZS12, HZS16, HZS17, HZS19 and
HZS20.

Border: Cut 8 strips 5½in (14cm) wide x
width of fabric in GP60TN. Join as necessary

and cut 2 strips 5½in x 72½in (14cm x
184.25cm) for the sides of the quilt and 2
strips 5½in x 76½in (14cm x 194.25cm) for
the top and bottom of the quilt.

Binding: Cut 8 strips 2½in (6.5cm) wide
across the width of the fabric in GP01GD.

Backing: Cut 2 pieces 40in x 84in (101.5cm
x 213.5cm) and 1 piece 11in x 84in (28cm x
213.5cm) in backing fabric.

MAKING THE QUILT
Use a ¼in (6mm) seam allowance throughout.
Referring to the quilt assembly diagram for
fabric placement, piece the patches into 8 rows
by colour. Join the rows to form the quilt centre.
Add side, then top and bottom borders as

indicated in the quilt assembly diagram.

FINISHING THE QUILT
Press the quilt top. Seam the backing pieces
using a ¼in (6mm) seam allowance to form a
piece approx. 90in x 84in (228.5cm x
213.5cm). Layer the quilt top, batting and
backing and baste together (see page 138).
Using toning machine quilting thread, quilt in
the ditch in the horizontal row joining seams,
then the long vertical seams. The squares are
quilted using variegated thread with an 'X'
shape that includes the previously unquilted
short rectangle seam. See the quilting
diagram. The borders are meander quilted,
free motion style following the paisley
pattern in the fabric print. Trim the quilt
edges and attach the binding (see page 139).

Quilting Diagram

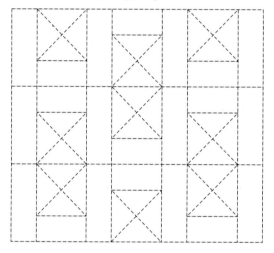

Yellow S Block Quilt ★★

Kaffe Fassett

The world of sunny yellows always intrigues me after seeing how the Chinese and Japanese use it so excitingly. We were lucky to find a tree in Christopher Lloyd's garden to show it to advantage. This simple to sew quilt could of course be done in any colourway that took your fancy. I've also done it in earthy browns but imagine it in pinks or some greens.

SIZE OF QUILT
The finished quilt will measure approx. 76in x 86in (193cm x 218.5cm).

MATERIALS
Patchwork and Border Fabrics:
ROMAN GLASS
Gold   GP01GD: ¼yd (25cm)
PAPERWEIGHT
Lime   GP20LM: ⅜ yd (35cm)
Pumpkin   GP20PN: ¼yd (25cm)
LOTUS LEAF
Yellow   GP29YE: ¼yd (25cm)
ZINNIA
Lime   GP31LM: ⅜yd (35cm)

CLOISONNE
Terracotta   GP46TC: ⅝ yd (60cm)
DAHLIA BLOOMS
Spring   GP54SP: ⅜yd (35cm)
FLOATING FLOWERS
Yellow   GP56YE: ⅜yd (35cm)
GUINEA FLOWER
Yellow   GP59YE: ½yd (45cm)
PAISLEY JUNGLE
Lime   GP60LM: 1⅜yds (1.25m)
              for outer border
Tangerine   GP60TN: ⅜yd (35cm)
JUNGLE STRIPE
Yellow   GP65YE: 1¼yds (1.15m)

PINKING FLOWER
Gold   GP66GD: 1¼yds (1.15cm)
              includes inner border
TARGETS
Pastel   GP67PT: ⅜yd (35cm)
BEKAH
Orange   GP69OR: ¼yd (25cm)
SPOT
Yellow   GP70YE: ⅜yd (35cm)
ABORIGINAL DOTS
Gold   GP71GD: ½yd (45cm)
Lime   GP71LM: ⅜yd (35cm)
Rose   GP71RO: ⅜yd (35cm)

Backing Fabric: 7½yds (6.9m)
We suggest these fabrics for backing:
PAPERWEIGHT Lime, GP20LM
LOTUS LEAF Yellow, GP29YE
PAISLEY JUNGLE Tangerine, GP60TN

Binding:
SPOT
Yellow   GP70YE: ¾yd (70cm)

Batting:
84in × 94in (213.5cm × 239cm).

Quilting thread:
Toning machine quilting thread.

Templates:

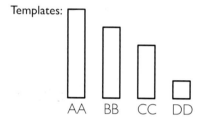

AA   BB   CC   DD

PATCH SHAPES
The 'S' blocks (finish to 10in (25.5cm) which
form the centre of this quilt are pieced using
3 rectangle patch shapes (Templates AA, BB
and CC) and a square patch shape
(Template DD). The blocks are pieced in 2
ways (see Block Diagrams). Block 2 is a
mirror image of block 1. The blocks are
straight set into rows and then surrounded
by 2 simple borders to complete the quilt.

CUTTING OUT
Cut the fabric in the order stated to prevent
waste, use leftover strips for later templates
as appropriate.
Fabric GP65YE ONLY: Cut 2½in (6.25cm)
strips down the length of the fabric
separating 4 different design elements. The
elements are cut as follows, please check the
photograph for help with this:
Design Element 1 – large blue/orange paisley:
Cut 1 of template AA, 4 of template BB, 1 of
template CC and 1 of template DD.
Design Element 2 – large lime paisley: Cut 3
of template AA, 6 of template BB, 3 of
template CC and 3 of template DD.
Design Element 3 – small paisley on blue:
Cut 3 of template AA, 6 of template BB, 3 of
template CC and 3 of template DD.
Design Element 4 – small paisley on orange:
Cut 2 of template AA, 8 of template BB, 2 of
template CC and 2 of template DD.
All Other Fabrics:
Template AA: Cut 2½in (6.25cm) strips
across the width of the fabric. Each strip will

give you 3 patches per width. Cut 4 in
GP59YE, 3 in GP46TC, GP60TN, GP71GD, 2
in GP20LM, GP31LM, GP56YE, GP66GD,
GP67PT, GP70YE, GP71LM, 1 in GP01GD,
GP20PN, GP29YE, GP54SP, GP69OR and
GP71RO.
Template BB: Cut 2½in (6.25cm) strips
across the width of the fabric. Each strip will
give you 4 patches per width. Cut 14 in
GP46TC, 12 in GP54SP, GP59YE, 10 in
GP20LM, GP31LM, GP71GD, GP71LM, 8 in
GP66GD, GP67PT, GP70YE, GP71RO, 6 in
GP01GD, GP20PN, GP29YE, GP56YE,
GP60TN and 4 in GP69OR.
Template CC: Cut 2½in (6.25cm) strips
across the width of the fabric or use leftover
strips from previous templates. Cut 4 in
GP59YE, 3 in GP46TC, GP60TN, GP71GD, 2
in GP20LM, GP31LM, GP56YE, GP66GD,
GP67PT, GP70YE, GP71LM, 1 in GP01GD,
GP20PN, GP29YE, GP54SP, GP69OR and
GP71RO.
Template DD: Cut 2½in (6.25cm) strips
across the width of the fabric or use leftover
strips from previous templates. Cut 4 in
GP59YE, 3 in GP46TC, GP60TN, GP71GD, 2
in GP20LM, GP31LM, GP56YE, GP66GD,
GP67PT, GP70YE, GP71LM, 1 in GP01GD,

GP20PN, GP29YE, GP54SP, GP69OR and
GP71RO.
Inner Border: Cut 7 strips 3½in (9cm) wide
across the width of fabric in GP66GD. Join as
necessary and cut 2 strips 3½in × 76½in
(9cm × 194.25cm) for the sides of the quilt
and 2 strips 3½in × 60½in (9cm × 153.75cm)
for the top and bottom of the quilt.
Outer Border: Cut 8 strips 5½in (14cm)
wide across the width of fabric in GP60LM.
Join as necessary and cut 2 strips 5½in ×
86½in (14cm × 219.75cm) for the sides of
the quilt and 2 strips 5½in × 66½in (14cm ×
169cm) for the top and bottom of the quilt.

Binding: Cut 9 strips 2½in (6.5cm) wide
across the width of the fabric in GP70YE.

Backing: Cut 2 pieces 40in × 84in (101.5cm
× 213.5cm) and 1 piece 15in × 84in (38cm ×
213.5cm) in backing fabric.

MAKING THE BLOCKS
Use a ¼in (6mm) seam allowance
throughout. Refer to the quilt assembly
diagram for fabric placement and block type.
Each block is made of a main fabric and a
background fabric. There are 2 block types,

Block Assembly Diagrams

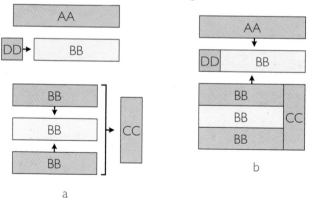

a

b

Block Diagrams

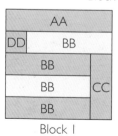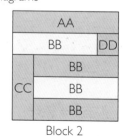

Block 1   Block 2

block 1 and block 2, as shown in the block diagrams. Follow block assembly diagrams a and b to piece 20 of Block 1. Use the same technique to piece 22 of block 2 which are a mirror image of block 1.

MAKING THE QUILT
Lay out the blocks as shown in the quilt assembly diagram. The blocks are rotated in alternating positions. Join the blocks into 7 rows of 6 blocks, then join the rows to form the quilt centre. Add the top and bottom inner borders, then side inner borders to the quilt centre as indicated in the quilt assembly diagram. Join the outer borders in the same way to complete the quilt.

FINISHING THE QUILT
Press the quilt top. Seam the backing pieces using a ¼in (6mm) seam allowance to form a piece approx. 84in × 94in (213.5cm × 239cm). Layer the quilt top, batting and backing and baste together (see page 138). Using toning machine quilting thread, quilt the blocks in the ditch. The inner border is quilted with 2 parallel lines offset from the seams by ¾in (2cm), in the outer border meander quilt following the paisley patterns in the fabric. Trim the quilt edges and attach the binding (see page 139).

Quilt Assembly Diagram

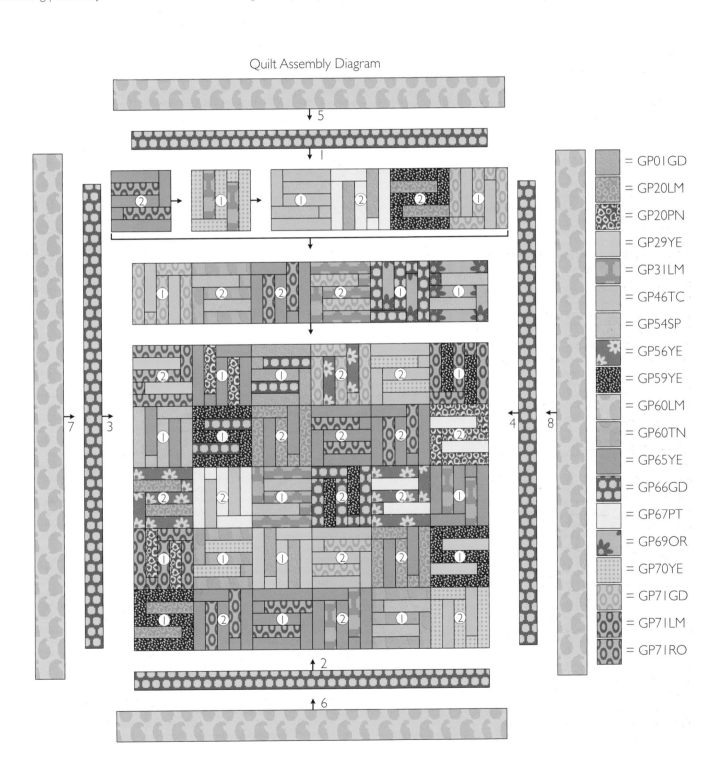

= GP01GD
= GP20LM
= GP20PN
= GP29YE
= GP31LM
= GP46TC
= GP54SP
= GP56YE
= GP59YE
= GP60LM
= GP60TN
= GP65YE
= GP66GD
= GP67PT
= GP69OR
= GP70YE
= GP71GD
= GP71LM
= GP71RO

Earthy S Block Quilt ★★

KAFFE FASSETT

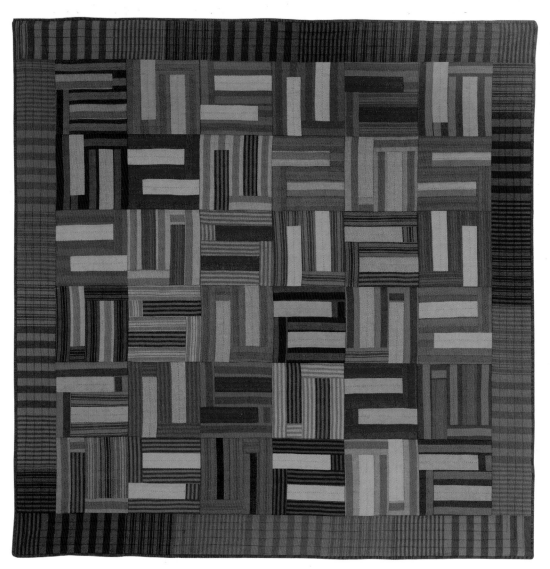

When I deepened this series of shot cotton stripes I envisaged using them in just such a quilt as this. The repetition of form shows off the subtle differences in the range of Tone Stripes. I started off with two of the very darkest stripes but took them out as they made the layout look drab. I also took out tangerine shot cotton and replaced it with clay for a much softer look.

SIZE OF QUILT
The finished quilt will measure approx. 71in × 71in (180.5cm × 180.5cm).

MATERIALS
Patchwork and Border Fabrics:
SHOT COTTON

Lavender	SC14:	⅜yd (35cm)
Mustard	SC16:	⅜yd (35cm)
Sage	SC17:	⅜yd (35cm)
Clay	SC60:	¼yd (25cm)

WOVEN TONE STRIPE

Citrus	WTSCN:	⅝yd (60cm)
Gold	WTSGD:	1yd (90cm)
Magenta	WTSMG:	⅝yd (60cm)
Moss	WTSMS:	⅝yd (60cm)
Ochre	WTSOC:	⅝yd (60cm)
Pumpkin	WTSPN:	1⅛yds (1m)
Purple	WTSPU:	¾yd (70cm)
Red	WTSRD:	⅝yd (60cm)
Spice	WTSSI:	⅝yd (60cm)
Suede	WTSSD:	1⅜yds (1.25m)

Backing Fabric: 4¾yds (4.35m)
Any of the WOVEN TONE STRIPE fabrics used in the quilt would be suitable for backing.

Binding:
WOVEN TONE STRIPE

Magenta	WTSMG:	¾yd (70cm)

Batting:
79in × 79in (201cm × 201cm).

Quilting thread:
Toning hand quilting thread.

Templates: See Yellow S Block Quilt

PATCH SHAPES
The 'S' blocks (finish to 10in (25.5cm) which form the centre of this quilt are pieced using 3 rectangle patch shapes (Templates AA, BB and CC) and a square patch shape (Template DD). The blocks are pieced in 2 ways (see Block Diagrams). Block 2 is a mirror image of block 1. The blocks are straight set into rows and then surrounded by a pieced border to complete the quilt.

SPECIAL CUTTING NOTES
The Woven Tone Stripe fabrics used in this

quilt have 3 different widths of stripe running along the length of the fabric. There are 2 sections of wide stripes at 12in (30.5cm) wide, 2 sections of medium stripes at 6in (15.25cm) wide and 2 sections of narrow stripes, 1 at 6in (15.25cm) wide and 1 at 3in wide (7.5cm) (along the selvedge). The borders are cut across the width of some of the fabrics, then the remaining fabric is used to cut the template shapes cut down the length of the fabric. We have given cutting instructions for each individual Woven Tone Stripe fabric separately.

CUTTING OUT
Cut the fabric in the order stated to prevent waste, use leftover strips for later templates as appropriate.
Shot Cotton Fabrics:
Template BB: Cut 2½in (6.25cm) strips across the width of the fabric. Each strip will give you 4 patches per width. Cut 14 in SC17, 12 in SC16, 10 in SC14 and 8 in SC60.
Border: Cut 6in (15.25cm) wide strips across the width of fabric so that the stripes run correctly. Check the photograph and quilt assembly diagram for help with this
For the left side border cut 1 strip 6in x 30in (15.25cm x 76.25cm) in WTSPN, 1 strip 6in x 25in (15.25cm x 63.5cm) in WTSGD and 1 strip 6in x 6½in (15.25cm x 16.5cm) in WTSSD.
For the right side border cut 1 strip 6in x 33½in (15.25cm x 85cm) in WTSSD and 1 strip 6in x 27½in (15.25cm x 70cm) in WTSPN.
For the top border cut 1 strip 6in x 20½in (15.25cm x 52cm) in WTSGD, 1 strip 6in x 29½in (15.25cm x 75cm) in WTSSD and 1 strip 6in x 22½in (15.25cm x 57.25cm) in WTSSD.
For the bottom border cut 1 strip 6in x 22½in (15.25cm x 57.25cm) in WTSSD, 1 strip 6in x 31in (15.25cm x 78.75cm) in WTSPN and 1 strip 6in x 19in (15.25cm x 48.25cm) in WTSGD.

Woven Tone Stripe Citrus, WTSCN
Wide Stripe: Cut 3 of Template AA, 6 of Template BB, 3 of Template CC and 3 of Template DD.
Medium Stripe: Cut 2 of Template BB.
Narrow Stripe: Cut 1 of Template AA, 2 of Template BB, 1 of Template CC and 1 of Template DD.

Woven Tone Stripe Gold, WTSGD
Cut borders first, see above.
Wide Stripe: Cut 4 of Template AA, 6 of

Template BB, 3 of Template CC and 4 of Template DD.
Medium Stripe: Cut 1 of Template AA, 4 of Template BB, 2 of Template CC and 1 of Template DD.
Narrow Stripe: Cut 1 of Template AA, 2 of Template BB, 1 of Template CC and 1 of Template DD.

Woven Tone Stripe Magenta, WTSMG
Wide Stripe: Cut 2 of Template AA, 6 of Template BB, 2 of Template CC and 2 of Template DD.
Medium Stripe: Cut 2 of Template BB.
Narrow Stripe: Cut 2 of Template BB.

Woven Tone Stripe Moss, WTSMS
Wide Stripe: Cut 4 of Template AA, 8 of Template BB, 4 of Template CC and 4 of Template DD.

Woven Tone Stripe Ochre, WTSOC
Wide Stripe: Cut 2 of Template AA, 10 of Template BB, 2 of Template CC and 2 of Template DD.
Medium Stripe: Cut 1 of Template AA, 2 of Template BB, 1 of Template CC and 1 of Template DD.
Narrow Stripe: Cut 1 of Template AA, 2 of Template BB, 1 of Template CC and 1 of Template DD.

Woven Tone Stripe Pumpkin, WTSPN
Cut borders first, see above.
Wide Stripe: Cut 3 of Template AA, 4 of Template BB, 3 of Template CC and 3 of Template DD.

Medium Stripe: Cut 2 of Template BB.

Woven Tone Stripe Purple, WTSPU
Wide Stripe: Cut 2 of Template AA, 6 of Template BB, 2 of Template CC and 2 of Template DD.
Medium Stripe: Cut 1 of Template AA, 2 of Template BB, 1 of Template CC and 1 of Template DD.
Narrow Stripe: Cut 8 of Template BB.

Woven Tone Stripe Red, WTSRD
Wide Stripe: Cut 1 of Template AA, 4 of Template BB, 1 of Template CC and 1 of Template DD.
Medium Stripe: Cut 2 of Template AA, 4 of Template BB, 2 of Template CC and 2 of Template DD.

Woven Tone Stripe Spice, WTSSI
Wide Stripe: Cut 1 of Template AA, 2 of Template BB, 1 of Template CC and 1 of Template DD.
Medium Stripe: Cut 1 of Template AA, 4 of Template BB, 1 of Template CC and 1 of Template DD.
Narrow Stripe: Cut 1 of Template AA, 2 of Template BB, 1 of Template CC and 1 of Template DD.

Woven Tone Stripe Suede, WTSSD
Cut borders first, see above.
Wide Stripe: Cut 2 of Template AA, 4 of Template BB, 2 of Template CC and 2 of Template DD.
Medium Stripe: Cut 1 of Template AA, 2 of Template BB, 1 of Template CC and 1 of

Quilting Diagram

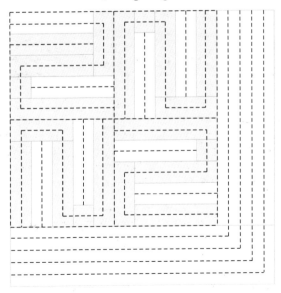

Template DD.
Narrow Stripe: Cut 1 of Template AA, 2 of Template BB, 1 of Template CC and 1 of Template DD.

Binding: Cut 8 strips 2½in (6.5cm) wide across the width of the fabric in WTSMG.

Backing: Cut 2 pieces 40in × 79in (101.5cm × 201cm) in backing fabric.

MAKING THE BLOCKS
Use a ¼in (6mm) seam allowance throughout. Refer to the quilt assembly diagram and photograph for fabric placement and block type. Each block is made of a main fabric and a background fabric. There are 2 block types, block 1 and block 2, as shown in the Yellow S Block Quilt block diagrams. Follow Yellow S Block Quilt block assembly diagrams a and b to piece 16 of Block 1. Use the same technique to piece 20 of block 2 which are a mirror image of block 1. Kaffe chose to use the same width of stripe for most blocks otherwise the pattern gets lost, however he occasionally chose to mix stripe widths for more variety.

MAKING THE QUILT
Lay out the blocks as shown in the quilt assembly diagram. The blocks are rotated in alternating positions. Join the blocks into 6 rows of 6 blocks, then join the rows to form the quilt centre. Join the borders as shown in the quilt assembly diagram. Add the side borders, then top and bottom borders to the quilt centre as indicated in the quilt assembly diagram to complete the quilt.

FINISHING THE QUILT
Press the quilt top. Seam the backing pieces using a ¼in (6mm) seam allowance to form a piece approx 79in × 79in (201cm × 201cm). Layer the quilt top, batting and backing and baste together (see page 138). Using toning hand quilting thread, quilt the blocks as shown in the quilting diagram. Quilt the border with parallel lines, offset by 1in, 2in, 3in and 4in (2.5cm, 5cm, 7.5cm and 10cm) from the seam. Trim the quilt edges and attach the binding (see page 139).

Quilt Assembly Diagram

Earthy S Block

= SC14
= SC16
= SC17
= SC60
= WTSCN
= WTSGD
= WTSMG
= WTSMS
= WTSOC
= WTSPN
= WTSPU
= WTSRD
= WTSSI
= WTSSD

Allotment Quilt ★

JANE BROCKET

Jane's simple quilt layout is inspired by the structure of an English allotment with rows of richly coloured plants in late summer.

SIZE OF QUILT
The finished quilt will measure approx.
99¾in x 88in (253.5cm x 223.5cm).

MATERIALS
Patchwork and Border Fabrics:
LOTUS LEAF
Umber   GP29UM: ⅛yd (15cm)
KIMONO
Crimson   GP33CM: ⅝ yd (60cm)
GUINEA FLOWER
Yellow   GP59YE: ⅜yd (35cm)
MINTON
Maroon   GP63MR: ½yd (45cm)
BROCADE FLORAL
Red   GP68RD: ⅝yd (60cm)

BEKAH
Magenta   GP69MG: ⅜yd (35cm)
Plum   GP69PL: ⅜yd (35cm)
SPOT
Burgundy   GP70BG: 1yd (90cm)
Fuchsia   GP70FU: ¼yd (25cm)
Magenta   GP70MG: ¼yd (25cm)
Red   GP70RD: ⅜yd (35cm)
Yellow   GP70YE: ¼yd (25cm)
ABORIGINAL DOTS
Lime   GP71LM: ⅜yd (35cm)
Rust   GP71RU: ⅜yd (35cm)
GERANIUM
Sage   PJ07SA: ⅝yd (60cm)
HOLLYHOCKS
Teal   PJ09TE: ⅝yd (60cm)

FOXGLOVES
Antique   PJ10AN: ⅝yd (60cm)
Red   PJ10RD: ½yd (45cm)
LUSCIOUS
Red   PJ11RD: 1⅞yds (1.7m)

Backing Fabric: 8⅝yds (7.9m)
We suggest these fabrics for backing:
KIMONO Crimson, GP33CM
GERANIUM Sage, PJ07SA
FOXGLOVES Antique, PJ10AN

Binding:
HOLLYHOCKS
Teal   PJ09TE: ⅞yd (80cm)

Batting:
108in x 96in (274.5cm x 244cm).

Quilting thread:
Dark red hand quilting thread.

PATCH SHAPES

This quilt is pieced from strips cut from the width of the fabric. The strips are pieced into 2 columns which are joined to form the quilt centre. The quilt centre is surrounded with 2 simple borders to complete the quilt.

CUTTING OUT

Inner Border: Cut 9 strips 2½in (6.25cm) wide across the width of fabric in GP70BG. Join as necessary and cut 2 strips 2½in x 89¼in (6.25cm x 226.75cm) for the sides of the quilt and 2 strips 2½in x 81½in (6.25cm x 207cm) for the top and bottom of the quilt. Reserve the remaining fabric for the quilt centre.

Outer Border: Cut 10 strips 4in (10.25cm) wide across the width of fabric in PJ11RD. Join as necessary and cut 2 strips 4in x 93¼in (10.25cm x 236.75cm) for the sides of the quilt and 2 strips 4in x 88½in (10.25cm x 224.75cm) for the top and bottom of the quilt. Reserve the remaining fabric for the quilt centre.

Quilt Centre:
Cut all strips across the width of the fabric, trim all to 39in (99cm) wide. We have listed strips to cut by fabric for easy cutting.
Lotus Leaf Umber, GP29UM: Cut 1 x 2½in (6.25cm) wide strip.
Kimono Crimson, GP33CM: Cut 1 x 5in (12.75cm), 1 x 4½in (11.5cm), 1 x 4in (10.25cm), 1 x 2in (5cm) wide strips.
Guinea Flower Yellow, GP59YE: Cut 1 x 3½in (9cm), 1 x 3in (7.5cm), 2 x 2in (5cm) wide strips.
Minton Maroon, GP63MR: Cut 1 x 5½in (14cm), 1 x 4½in (11.5cm), 1 x 4in (10.25cm) wide strips.
Brocade Floral Red, GP68RD: Cut 1 x 7½in (19cm), 1 x 5in (12.75cm), 2 x 2in (5cm) wide strips.
Bekah Magenta, GP69MG: Cut 1 x 4½in (11.5cm), 1 x 3¾in (9.5cm), 1 x 2in (5cm) wide strips.
Bekah Plum, GP69PL: Cut 1 x 5in (12.75cm), 1 x 3½in (9cm), 1 x 3in (7.5cm) wide strips.
Spot Burgundy, GP70BG: Cut 1 x 2½in (6.25cm), 3 x 2in (5cm) wide strips.
Spot Fuchsia, GP70FU: Cut 3 x 2in (5cm) wide strips.
Spot Magenta, GP70MG: 1 x 2¼in (5.75cm),

1 x 2in (5cm) wide strips.
Spot Red, GP70RD: Cut 2 x 2½in (6.25cm), 2 x 2in (5cm) wide strips.
Spot Yellow, GP70YE: Cut 1 x 2¼in (5.75cm), 2 x 2in (5cm) wide strips.
Aboriginal Dots Lime, GP71LM: Cut 1 x 2½in (6.25cm), 2 x 2in (5cm), 1 x 1¾in (4.5cm), 1 x 1½in (3.75cm) wide strips.
Aboriginal Dots Rust, GP71RU: Cut 2 x 3in (7.5cm), 1 x 1½in (3.75cm) wide strips.
Geranium Sage, PJ07SA: Cut 1 x 4½in (11.5cm), 1 x 4¼in (10.75cm), 1 x 3in (7.5cm), 2 x 2½in (6.25cm) wide strips.
Hollyhocks Teal, PJ09TE: Cut 1 x 7¼in (18.5cm), 1 x 4½in (11.5cm), 1 x 3½in (9cm) wide strips.
Foxgloves Antique, PJ10AN: Cut 1 x 4½in (11.5cm), 1 x 3¾in (9.5cm), 1 x 3in (7.5cm), 1 x 2½in (6.25cm), 1 x 2¼in (5.75cm) wide strips.
Foxgloves Red, PJ10RD: Cut 1 x 5in (12.75cm), 1 x 4½in (11.5cm), 1 x 3½in (9cm) wide strips.
Luscious Red, PJ11RD: Cut 2 x 5in (12.75cm), 1 x 4in (10.25cm), 1 x 3½in (9cm) wide strips.

Binding: Cut 10 strips 2½in (6.5cm) wide across the width of the fabric in PJ09TE.

Backing: Cut 2 pieces 40in x 96in (101.5cm x 244cm) and 1 piece 29in x 96in (73.75 x 244cm) in backing fabric.

MAKING THE QUILT CENTRE

Use a ¼in (6mm) seam allowance throughout. The quilt assembly diagram shows the position of the fabrics and strip widths for each column. Join the strips together in order, stitching left to right for the first seam, then right to left for the second and so on, alternating direction for each row. This helps to prevent warping. When both columns are complete join at the centre to form the quilt centre.

ADDING THE BORDERS

Join the side, then top and bottom inner borders to the quilt centre. Join the outer borders in the same manner, as shown in the border assembly diagram.

FINISHING THE QUILT

Press the quilt top. Seam the backing pieces using a ¼in (6mm) seam allowance to form a piece approx. 108in x 96in (274.5cm x 244cm). Layer the quilt top, batting and backing and baste together (see page 137). Using dark red hand quilting thread, quilt parallel lines across the quilt about 4in (10.25cm) apart and offset from any seams by ¼in (6mm). Trim the quilt edges and attach the binding (see page 138).

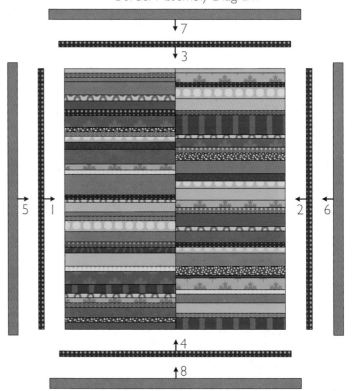

Border Assembly Diagram

Quilt Centre Assembly Diagram

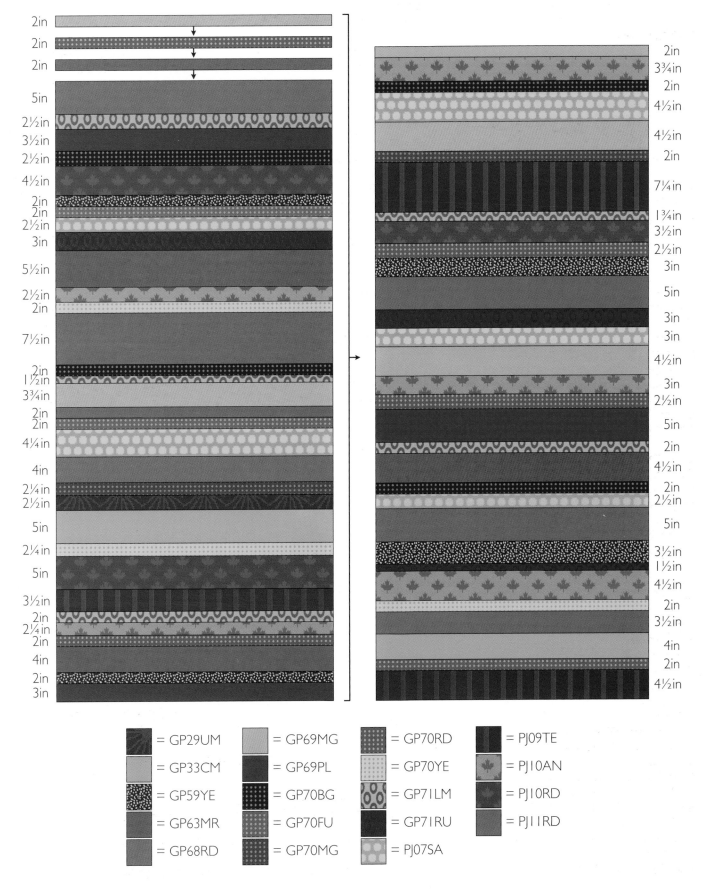

= GP29UM	= GP70RD
= GP33CM	= GP70YE
= GP59YE	= GP71LM
= GP63MR	= GP71RU
= GP68RD	= PJ07SA
= GP69MG	= PJ09TE
= GP69PL	= PJ10AN
= GP70BG	= PJ10RD
= GP70FU	= PJ11RD
= GP70MG	

Bekah's Basket Sampler Quilt ★ ★ ★

BETSY RICKLES

The quilt centre with brightly coloured baskets has a formal almost Elizabethan feel, which contrasts with the informal border. Kaffe's lime Paperweight for the background gives a contemporary twist.

SIZE OF QUILT
The finished quilt will measure approx.
84in x 84in (213.5cm x 213.5cm).

MATERIALS
Patchwork Fabrics:
ROMAN GLASS
Red	GP01RD:	⅜yd (35cm)

PAPERWEIGHT
Lime	GP20LM:	5yds (4.6m)
Paprika	GP20PP:	⅜yd (35cm)

LOTUS LEAF
Red	GP29RD:	⅛yd (15cm)
Wine	GP29WN:	⅜yd (35cm)
Yellow	GP29YE:	⅛yd (15cm)

ZINNIA
Crimson	GP31CR:	¼yd (25cm)
Lime	GP31LM:	⅛yd (15cm)

KIMONO
Crimson/Magenta	GP33CM:	⅛yd (15cm)

CLOISONNE
Magenta	GP46MG:	⅜yd (35cm)

FLOWER BASKET
Magenta	GP48MG:	⅝yd (60cm)

PAPER FANS
Red	GP57RD:	¼yd (25cm)

GUINEA FLOWER
Pink	GP59PK:	⅛yd (15cm)

PAISLEY JUNGLE
Rust	GP60RU:	¾yd (70cm)

JUNGLE STRIPE
Dark	GP65DK:	¼yd (25cm)
Red	GP65RD:	⅛yd (15cm)

Yellow GP65YE: ⅛yd (15cm)
PINKING FLOWER
Red GP66RD: ⅜yd (35cm)
TARGETS
Pastel GP67PT: ¼yd (25cm)
Red GP67RD: ⅜yd (35cm)
BROCADE FLORAL
Red GP68RD: ¼yd (25cm)
Verdigris GP68VE: ⅛yd (15cm)
BEKAH
Magenta GP69MG: ⅝yd (60cm)
Orange GP69OR: ¾yd (70cm)
ABORIGINAL DOTS
Lime GP71LM: ¼yd (25cm)

Backing Fabric: 6¾yds (6.2m)
We suggest these fabrics for backing:
LOTUS LEAF Yellow, GP29YE
BEKAH Magenta, GP69MG
BEKAH Orange, GP69OR

Binding:
BEKAH
Orange GP69OR: ¾yd (70cm).

Batting:
92in × 92in (223.5cm × 223.5cm)

Quilting thread:
Toning machine quilting thread.

Other Materials:
Lightweight adhesive web.

Appliqué thread:
Matching cotton thread for the handles.
Toning/contrasting machine embroidery thread for appliqué circles.

Templates:

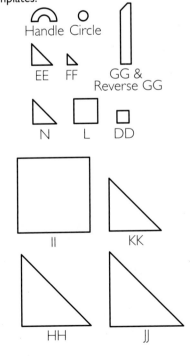

Handle Circle

EE FF GG & Reverse GG

N L DD

II KK

HH JJ

PATCH SHAPES
The quilt centre is made of pieced basket blocks which uses 3 triangle patch shapes (Templates EE, FF and HH) and 1 lozenge patch shape (GG & Reverse GG). The blocks also have hand appliquéd handles (Handle) and machine appliquéd 'fruit' circles (Circle) applied. The blocks are set on point alternated with a square patch shape (Template II) which also has 'fruit' circles machine appliquéd. The edges and corners of the quilt centre are filled using 2 more triangle patch shapes (Templates JJ and KK). The quilt centre is surrounded with a series of 3 pieced borders. These borders are pieced using 2 square patch shapes (Templates L and DD) and 1 triangle patch shape (Template N). Some of the templates for this quilt are printed at 50% of true size, photocopy at 200% before using.

CUTTING OUT
Cut the fabric in the order stated to prevent waste, we suggest drawing around the larger templates to get the best fit for fabric GP20LM

Template JJ: Cut 2 × 18⅞in (48cm) squares in GP20LM, cut each square twice diagonally to make 4 triangles using the template as a guide, this will ensure that the long side of the triangle will not have a bias edge. Note: do not move the patches until both diagonals have been cut. Total 8 triangles.
Template II: Cut 4 × 13in (33cm) squares in GP20LM.
Template HH: Cut 5 × 12⅞in (32.75cm) squares in GP20LM, cut each square diagonally to make 2 triangles using the template as a guide. Total 9 triangles (1 spare).
Template KK: Cut 2 × 9⅝in (24.5cm) squares in GP20LM, cut each square diagonally to make 2 triangles using the template as a guide. Total 4 triangles.
Template EE: Cut 5 × 4⅛in (10.5cm) squares in GP20LM, cut each square diagonally to make 2 triangles using the template as a guide. Total 9 triangles (1 spare).
Template GG & reverse GG: Cut 2⅛in (5.5cm) strips across the width of the fabric. Each strip will give you 4 patches per width. Cut 9 in GP20LM. Flip the template over and cut 9 Reverse GG shapes in GP20LM. Total 18 shapes.
Template FF: Cut 2½in (6.25cm) strips across the width of the fabric. Each strip will give you 32 patches per width. Cut 135 in GP20LM, 92 in GP60RU, 23 in GP29WN, GP46MG, GP48MG, GP66RD and GP69MG. Total 342 triangles.

Template N: Cut 4⅞in (12.5cm) strips across the width of the fabric. Each strip will give you 16 patches per width. Cut 79 in GP20LM, 8 in GP01RD, GP29WN, GP46MG, GP57RD, GP60RU, GP69MG, 7 in GP20PP, 6 in GP31CR, GP67RD and 5 in GP66RD. Total 158 triangles.
Template L: Cut 4½in (11.5cm) strips across the width of the fabric. Each strip will give you 8 patches per width. Cut 21 in GP69OR, 20 in GP20LM, 8 in GP67PT, 4 in GP46MG, GP57RD, GP60RU, GP69MG, 3 in GP29WN, GP31CR, 2 in GP01RD, GP66RD, GP67RD and 1 in GP48MG. Total 78 squares.
Template DD: Cut 2½in (6.25cm) strips across the width of the fabric. Each strip will give you 16 patches per width. Cut 191 in GP20LM, 22 in GP68RD, 20 in GP71LM, 19 in GP48MG, GP69MG, 15 in GP01RD, GP20PP, 14 in GP31LM, GP46MG, GP67RD, 13 in GP29RD, GP33CM, GP59PK, GP65YE, 12 in GP60RU, GP65RD, 11 in GP66RD, 10 in GP69OR, 8 in GP67PT, 6 in GP68VE, 5 in GP29YE and 1 in GP29WN. Total 460 squares.
Appliqué Basket Handles: Cut 8 in GP60RU, 2 in GP29WN, GP46MG, GP48MG, GP66RD and GP69MG. Total 18 handles.
Appliqué Circles: Trace the circles onto the paper side of your adhesive web leaving a ¼in (6mm) gap between the shapes. Roughly cut out the circles about ⅛in (3mm) outside your drawn line. Bond the shapes to REVERSE of the fabrics. Bond 42 circles in GP69MG, 18 in GP48MG, GP60RU and 12 in GP65DK. Cut out the circles with very sharp scissors. Total 90 circles.

Backing: Cut 2 pieces 40in × 92in (101.5cm × 233.5cm), 2 pieces 40in × 13in (101.5cm × 33cm) and 1 piece 13in × 13in (33cm × 33cm) in backing fabric.

Binding: Cut 9 strips 2½in (6.5cm) wide across the width of the fabric in GP69OR.

MAKING THE BLOCKS
Use a ¼in (6mm) seam allowance throughout. Refer to the quilt centre assembly diagram for fabric placement. Piece the bottom half of a basket block as shown in block assembly diagram a, b and c. Hand appliqué the handles to a template HH triangle, positioning them as shown on the template, there is no need to turn under the bottom edges as they will be caught in the centre block seam. Remove the backing paper from the appliqué circles and position carefully as shown on the template. Bond the

circles into place and machine appliqué with a fine satin stitch or blanket stitch. The stitching should sit mostly on the bonded shape. Join the 2 parts of the basket block as shown in block assembly diagram d. The finished block can be seen in diagram e. Make 9 basket blocks.

Take a template II square and machine appliqué 9 circles positioned as shown on the template. Make 4.

MAKING THE QUILT CENTRE
Lay out the basket blocks alternated with the template II squares as shown in the

quilt centre assembly diagram. Fill in the edges with template JJ triangles and the corners with template KK triangles. Separate into diagonal rows and join. Join the rows to form the quilt centre. Trim the centre evenly to 52½in (133.5cm) square if necessary.

Basket Block Assembly Diagrams

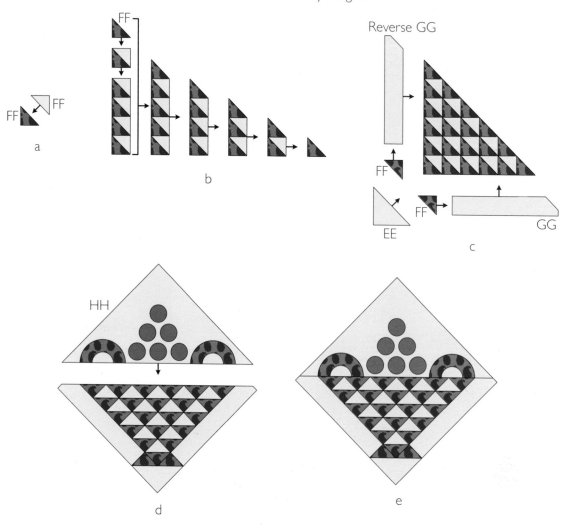

Border Block Assembly Diagrams

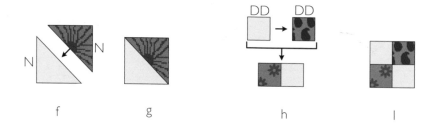

MAKING THE BORDERS

The borders are pieced from a selection of 4in (10.25cm) finished size blocks. There are plain 4½in (11.5cm) cut size squares (template L), half square triangle blocks, pieced as shown in border block assembly diagram f, the finished block is shown in diagram g and 4 patch blocks pieced as shown in diagram h with the finished block shown in diagram i. We have shown the layout of blocks and fabrics accurately in the border assembly diagram, but the exact placement of blocks is not important The only important thing to note is the general positioning of the GP20LM 'background' fabric which sets the checkerboard effect,

however there are places where this is broken by using other fabrics and this adds to the charm and sparkle of the quilt.

The inner border is pieced mostly from 4 patch blocks. Piece 2 sections 13 blocks x 2 blocks and join them to the sides of the quilt, then piece 2 sections 17 blocks x 2 blocks and join to the top and bottom of the quilt.

The middle border is pieced mostly from template L squares. Piece 2 sections 17 blocks x 1 block and join them to the sides of the quilt, then piece 2 sections 19 blocks x 1 block and join to the top and bottom of the quilt. The outer border is pieced mostly from half

square triangle blocks. Piece 2 sections 19 blocks x 1 block and join them to the sides of the quilt, then piece 2 sections 21 blocks x 1 block and join to the top and bottom to complete the quilt.

FINISHING THE QUILT

Press the quilt top. Seam the backing pieces using a ¼in (6mm) seam allowance to form a piece approx. 92in x 92in (223.5cm x 223.5cm). Layer the quilt top, batting and backing and baste together (see page 138). Using toning machine quilting thread, quilt a meander pattern across the surface of the quilt. Trim the quilt edges and attach the binding (see page 139).

Quilt Centre Assembly Diagram

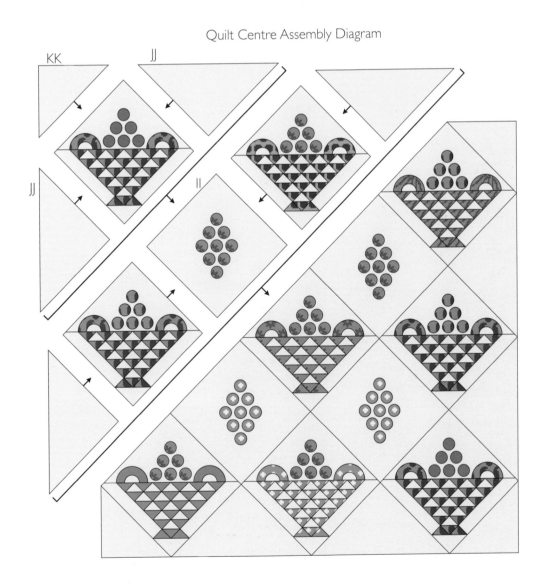

Border Assembly Diagram

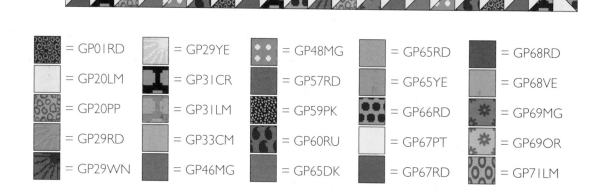

L

11
7
3
4
8
12
9
5
1
2
6
10

= GP01RD	= GP29YE	= GP48MG	= GP65RD	= GP68RD
= GP20LM	= GP31CR	= GP57RD	= GP65YE	= GP68VE
= GP20PP	= GP31LM	= GP59PK	= GP66RD	= GP69MG
= GP29RD	= GP33CM	= GP60RU	= GP67PT	= GP69OR
= GP29WN	= GP46MG	= GP65DK	= GP67RD	= GP71LM

TEMPLATES

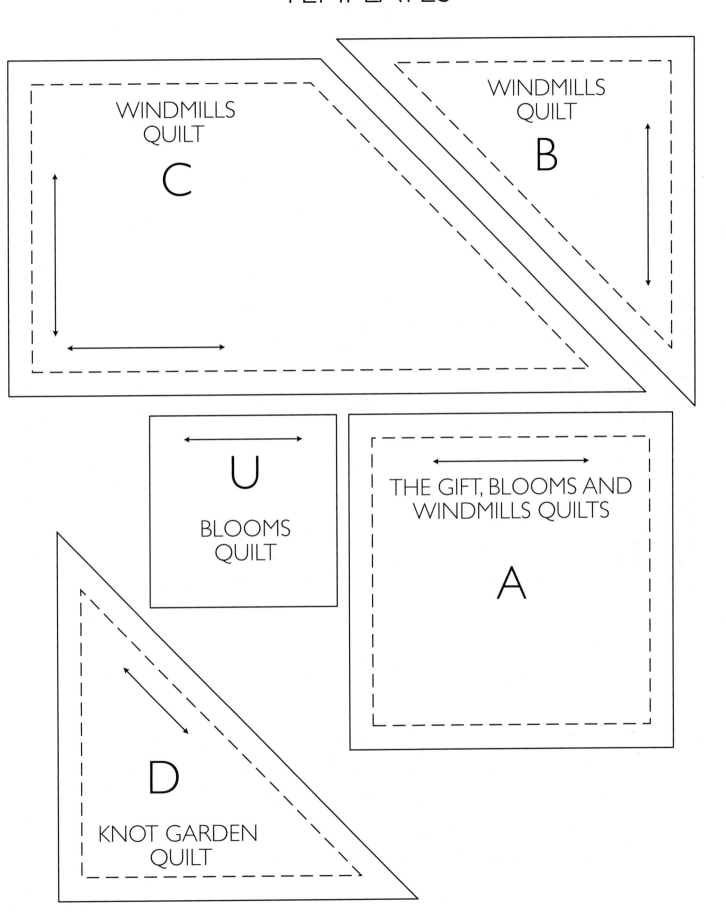

WINDMILLS
QUILT

C

WINDMILLS
QUILT

B

U

BLOOMS
QUILT

THE GIFT, BLOOMS AND
WINDMILLS QUILTS

A

D

KNOT GARDEN
QUILT

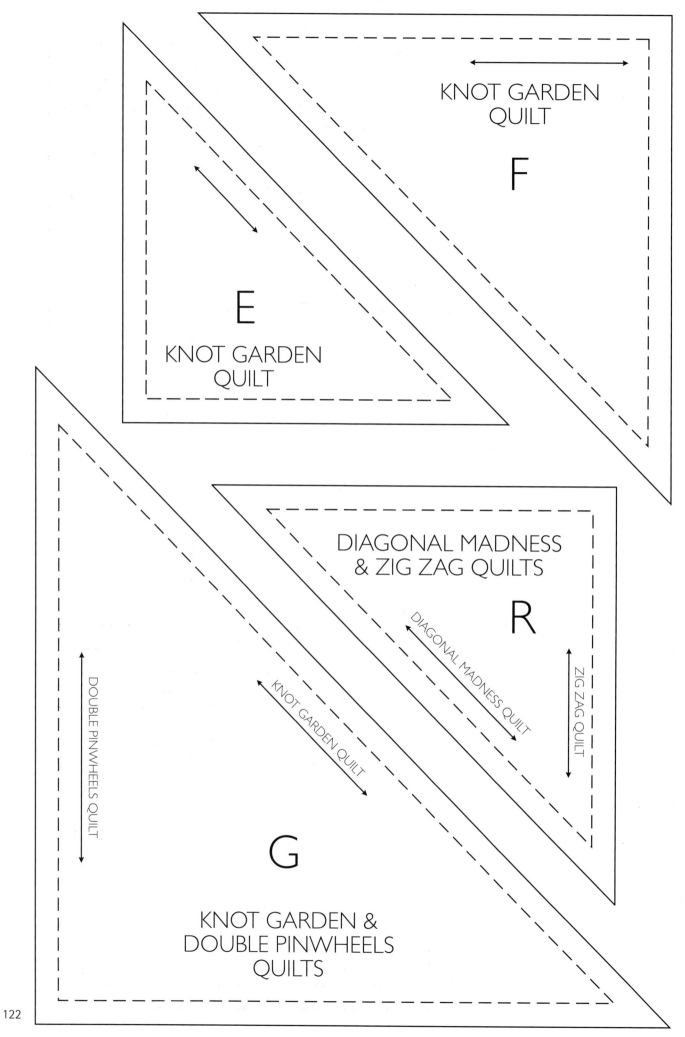

KNOT GARDEN
QUILT

F

E
KNOT GARDEN
QUILT

DIAGONAL MADNESS
& ZIG ZAG QUILTS

R

DIAGONAL MADNESS QUILT

ZIG ZAG QUILT

DOUBLE PINWHEELS QUILT

KNOT GARDEN QUILT

G

KNOT GARDEN &
DOUBLE PINWHEELS
QUILTS

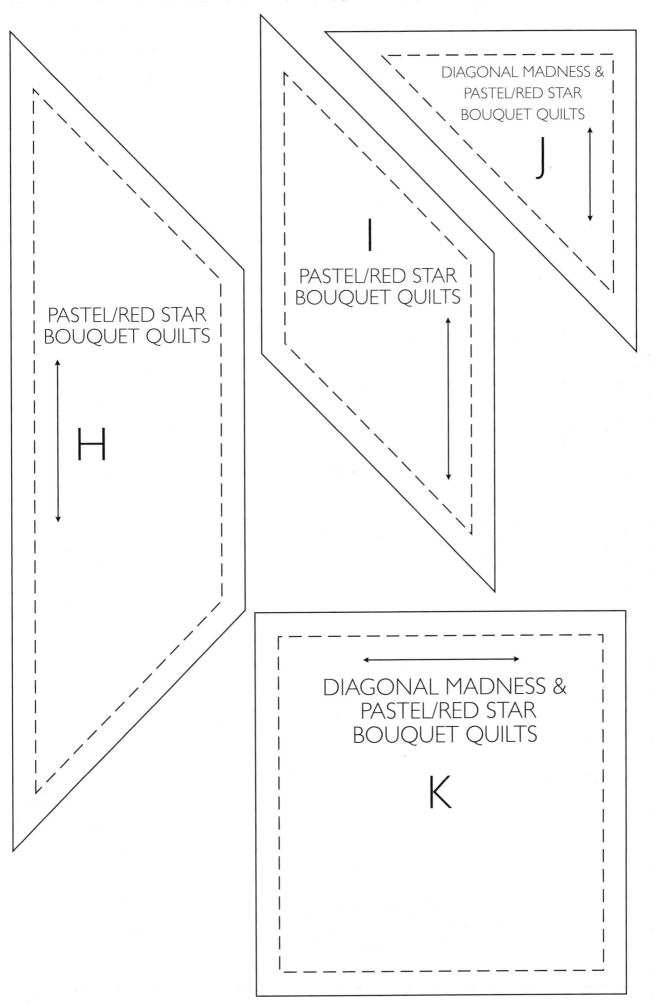

PASTEL/RED STAR
BOUQUET QUILTS

H

I

PASTEL/RED STAR
BOUQUET QUILTS

DIAGONAL MADNESS &
PASTEL/RED STAR
BOUQUET QUILTS

J

DIAGONAL MADNESS &
PASTEL/RED STAR
BOUQUET QUILTS

K

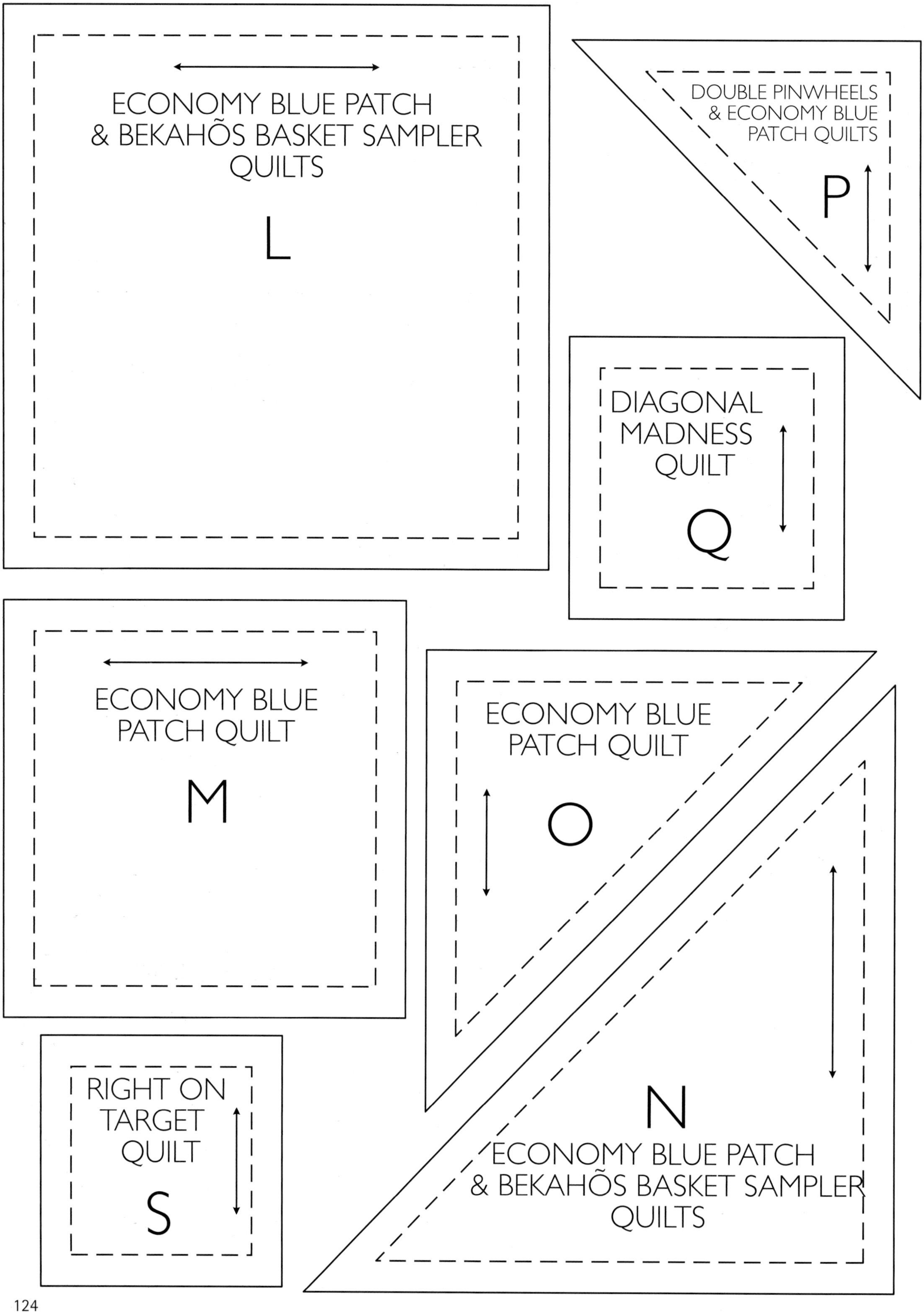

ECONOMY BLUE PATCH
& BEKAHÕS BASKET SAMPLER
QUILTS

L

DOUBLE PINWHEELS
& ECONOMY BLUE
PATCH QUILTS

P

DIAGONAL
MADNESS
QUILT

Q

ECONOMY BLUE
PATCH QUILT

M

ECONOMY BLUE
PATCH QUILT

O

N

ECONOMY BLUE PATCH
& BEKAHÕS BASKET SAMPLER
QUILTS

RIGHT ON
TARGET
QUILT

S

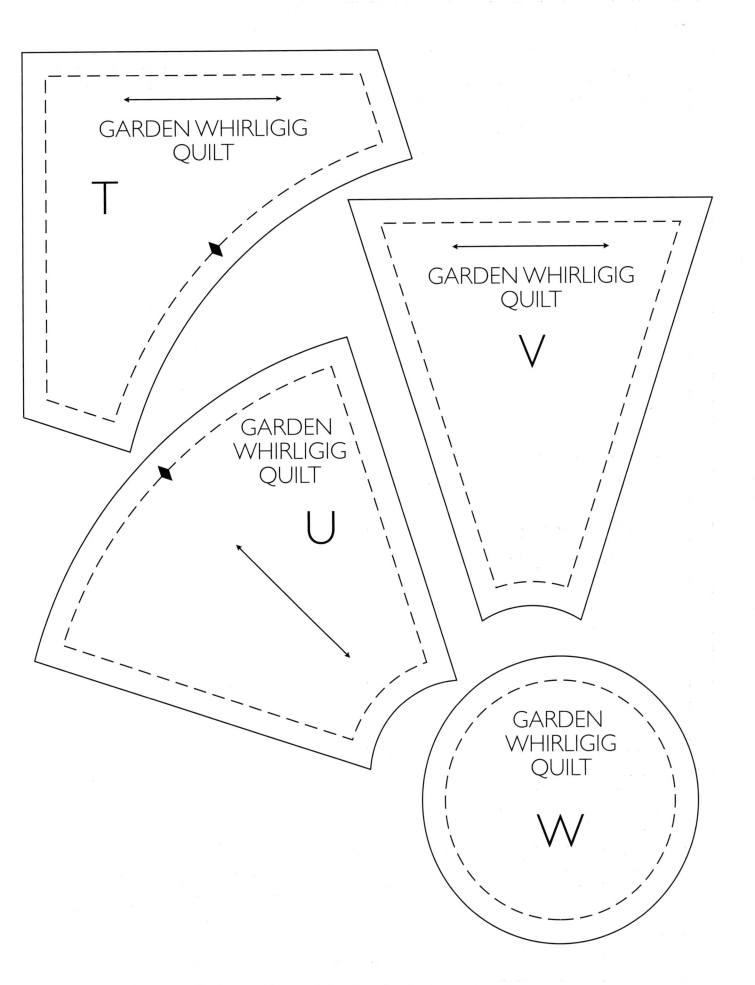

GARDEN WHIRLIGIG
QUILT

T

GARDEN WHIRLIGIG
QUILT

V

GARDEN
WHIRLIGIG
QUILT

U

GARDEN
WHIRLIGIG
QUILT

W

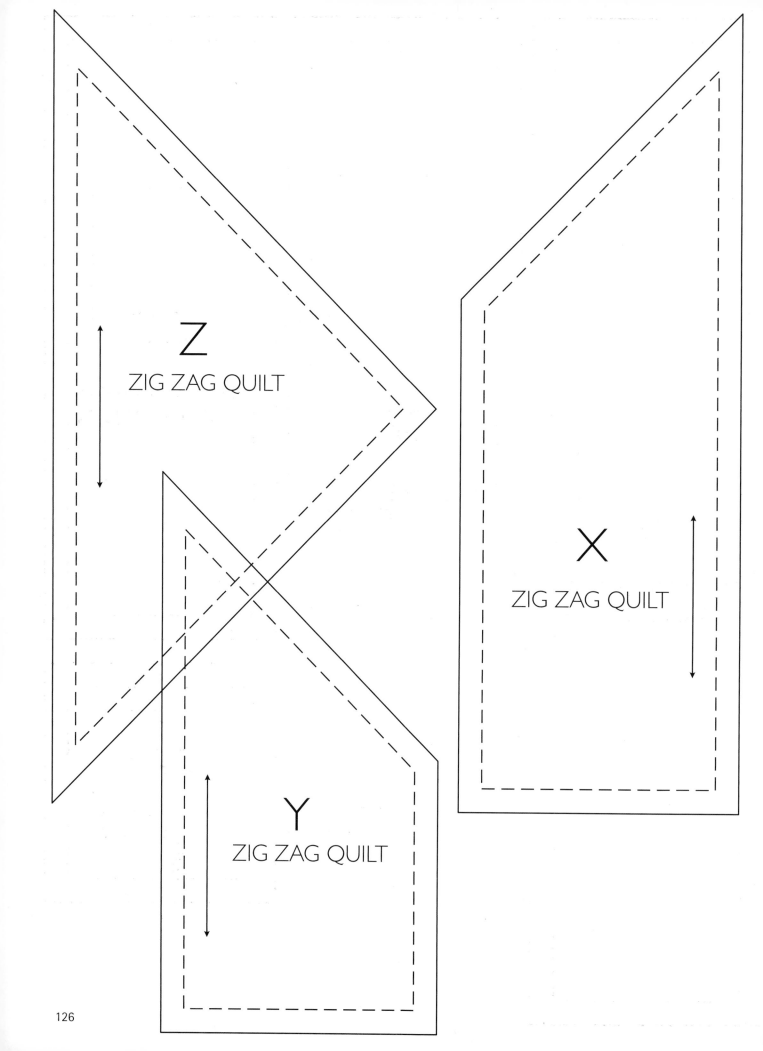

Z
ZIG ZAG QUILT

X
ZIG ZAG QUILT

Y
ZIG ZAG QUILT

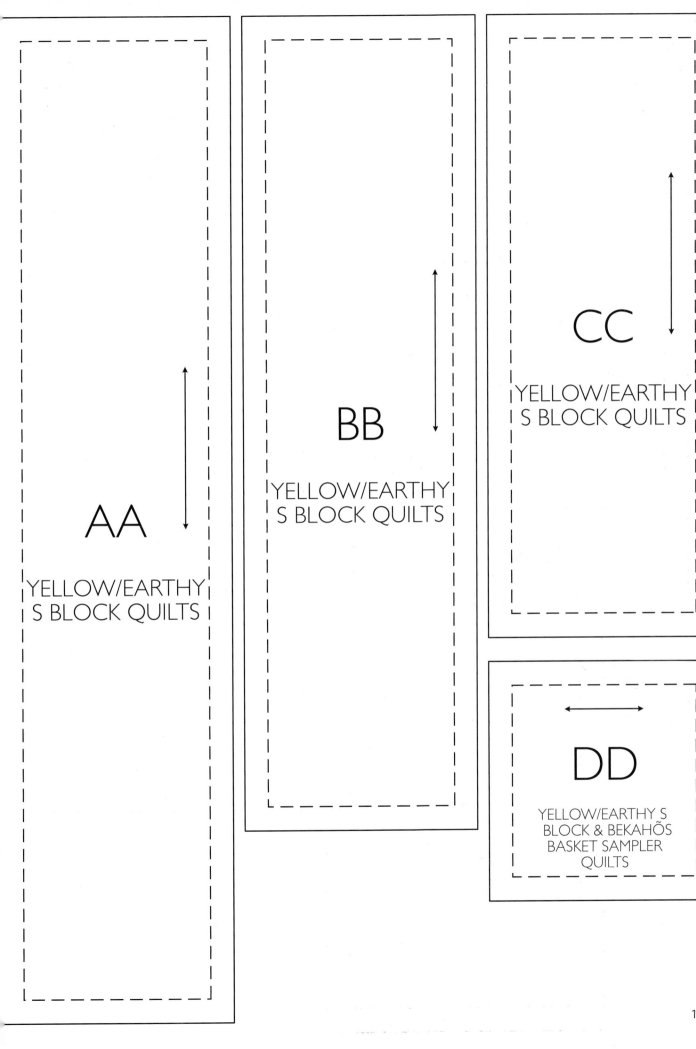

AA

YELLOW/EARTHY
S BLOCK QUILTS

BB

YELLOW/EARTHY
S BLOCK QUILTS

CC

YELLOW/EARTHY
S BLOCK QUILTS

DD

YELLOW/EARTHY S
BLOCK & BEKAHÕS
BASKET SAMPLER
QUILTS

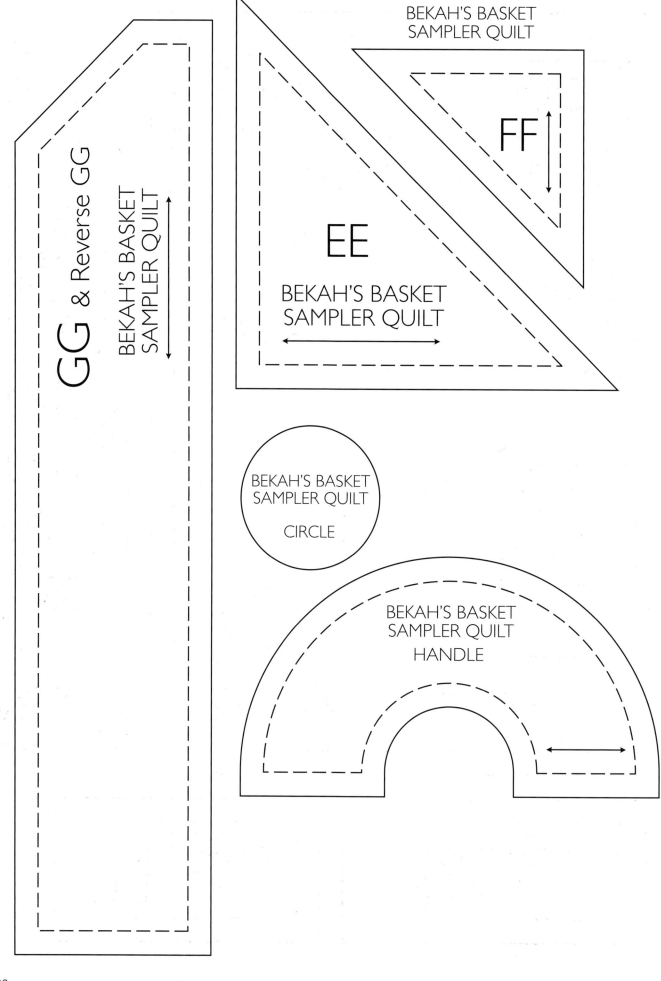

GG & Reverse GG

BEKAH'S BASKET SAMPLER QUILT

BEKAH'S BASKET SAMPLER QUILT

FF

EE

BEKAH'S BASKET SAMPLER QUILT

BEKAH'S BASKET SAMPLER QUILT

CIRCLE

BEKAH'S BASKET SAMPLER QUILT

HANDLE

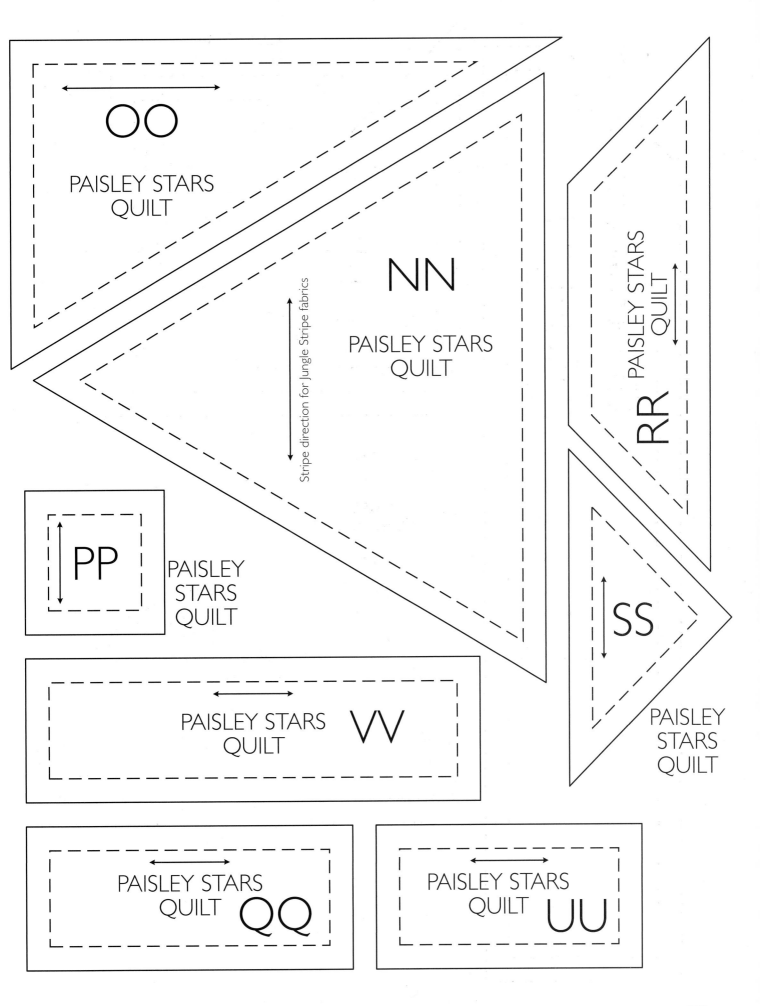

OO
PAISLEY STARS
QUILT

NN
PAISLEY STARS
QUILT

Stripe direction for Jungle Stripe fabrics

PP
PAISLEY
STARS
QUILT

VV
PAISLEY STARS
QUILT

RR
PAISLEY STARS
QUILT

SS
PAISLEY
STARS
QUILT

QQ
PAISLEY STARS
QUILT

UU
PAISLEY STARS
QUILT

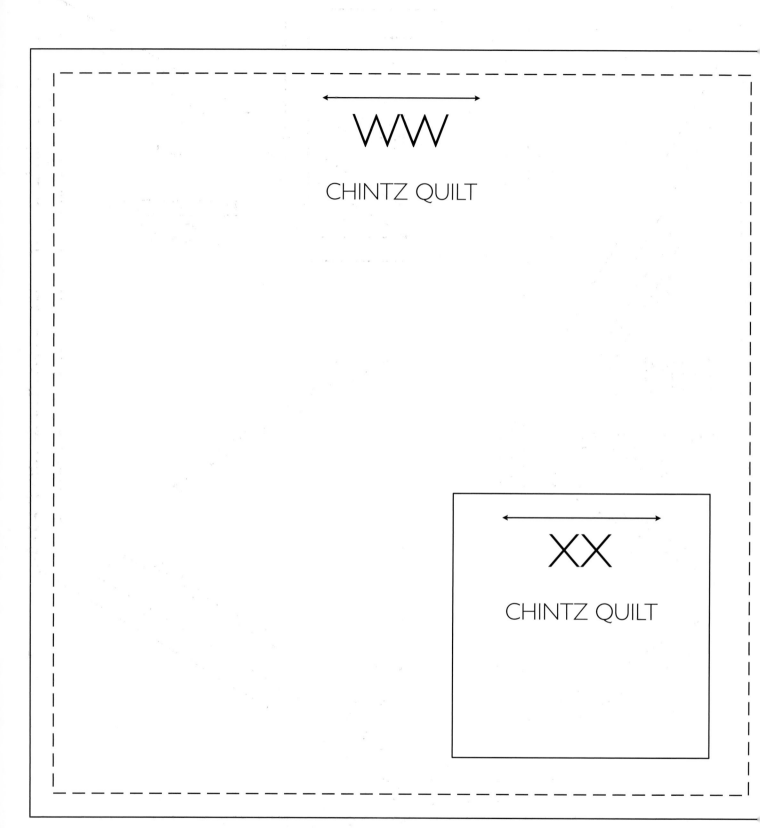

WW

CHINTZ QUILT

XX

CHINTZ QUILT

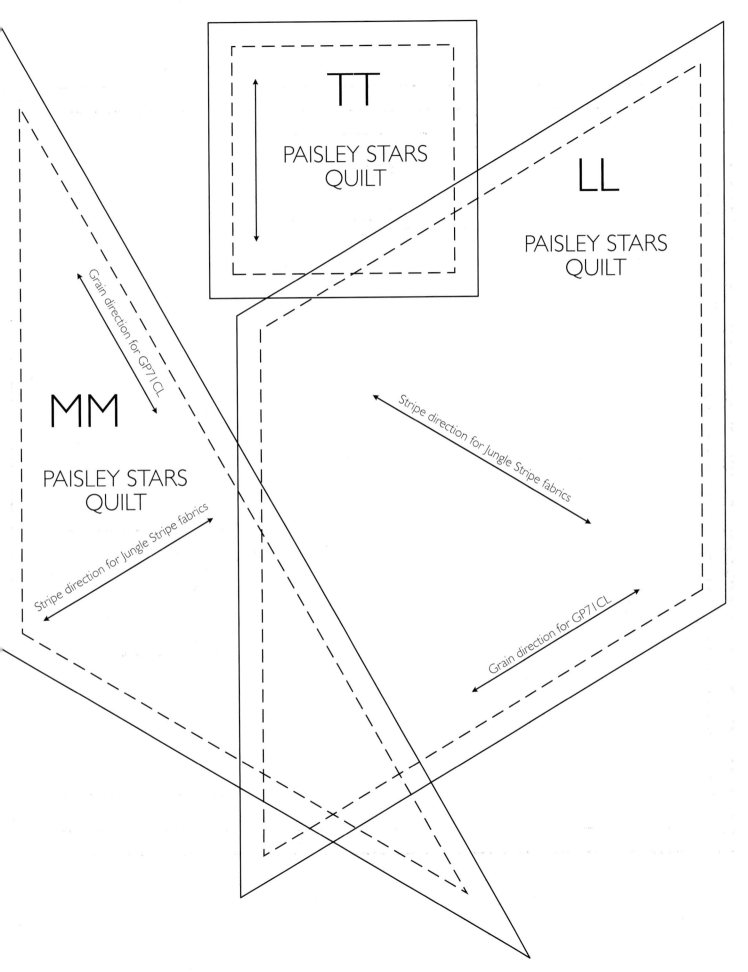

TT

PAISLEY STARS
QUILT

LL

PAISLEY STARS
QUILT

Grain direction for GP71CL

MM

PAISLEY STARS
QUILT

Stripe direction for Jungle Stripe fabrics

Stripe direction for Jungle Stripe fabrics

Grain direction for GP71CL

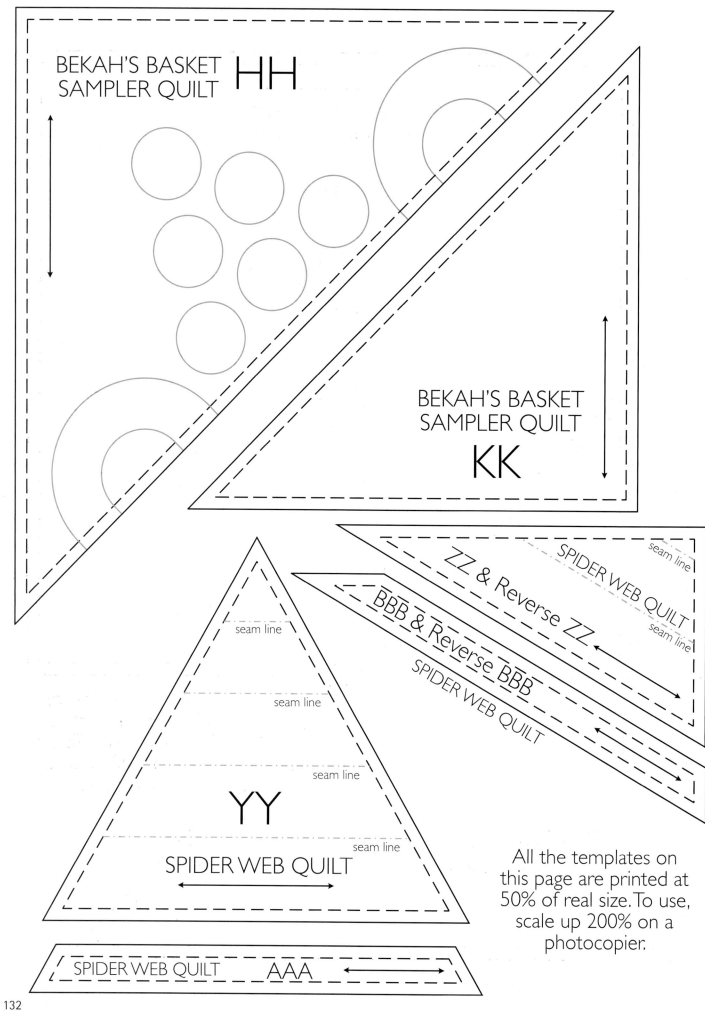

BEKAH'S BASKET
SAMPLER QUILT **HH**

BEKAH'S BASKET
SAMPLER QUILT

KK

SPIDER WEB QUILT seam line
ZZ & Reverse ZZ
seam line

BBB & Reverse BBB
SPIDER WEB QUILT

seam line

seam line

seam line

YY

seam line

SPIDER WEB QUILT

All the templates on
this page are printed at
50% of real size. To use,
scale up 200% on a
photocopier.

SPIDER WEB QUILT **AAA**

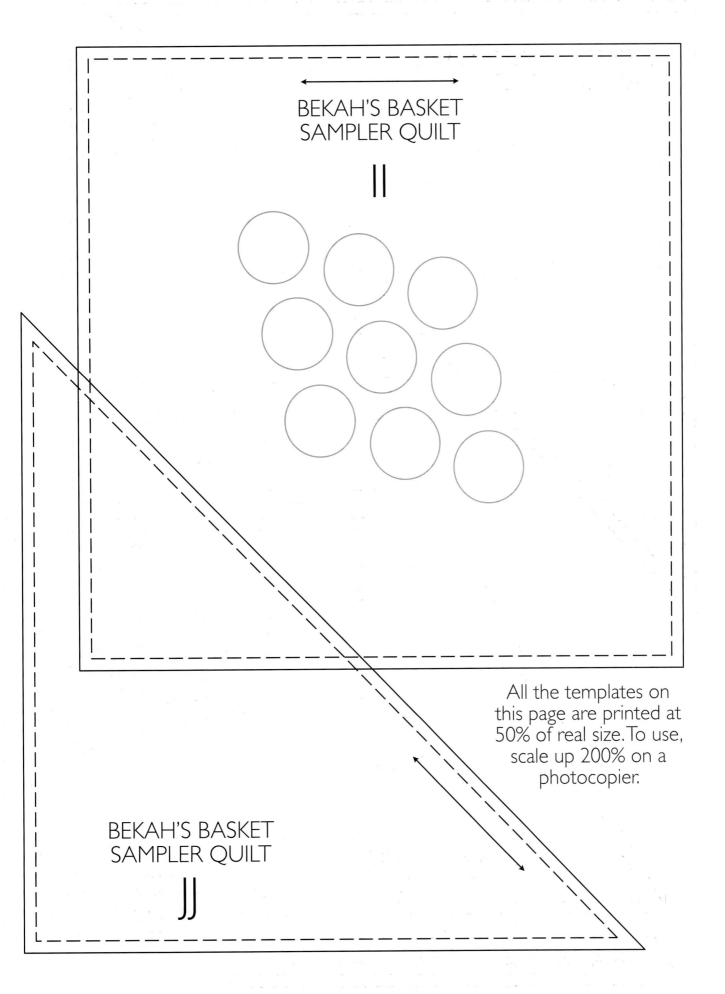

BEKAH'S BASKET
SAMPLER QUILT

II

BEKAH'S BASKET
SAMPLER QUILT

JJ

All the templates on
this page are printed at
50% of real size. To use,
scale up 200% on a
photocopier.

THE GIFT QUILT
APPLIQUÉ SHAPES
These shapes are printed
at 50% of real size.
To use, scale them
up 200% on a
photocopier

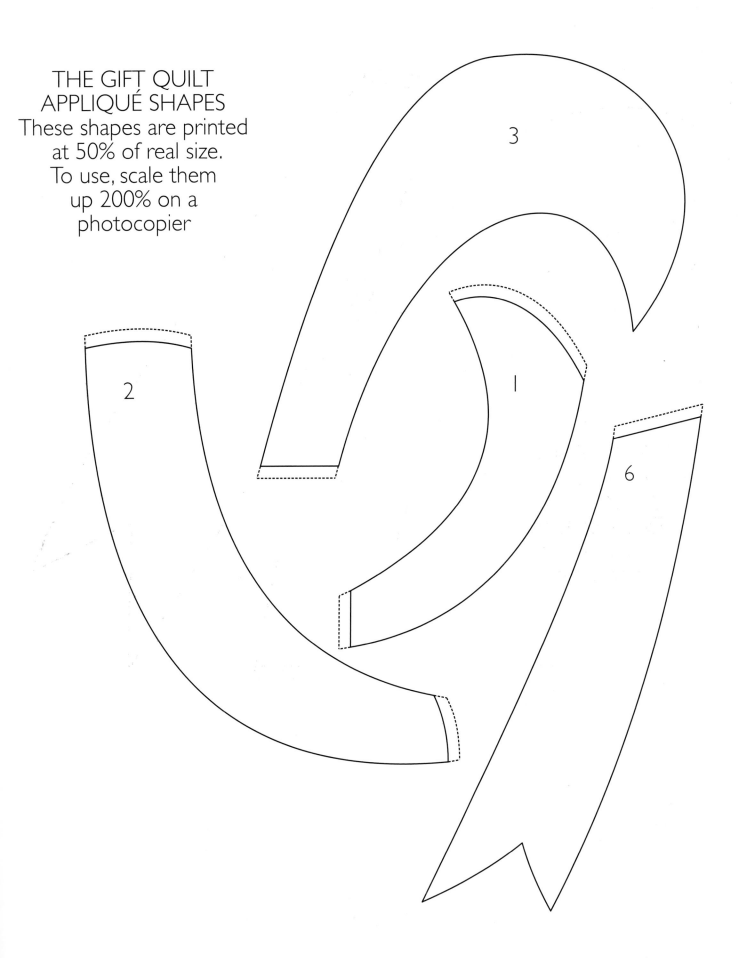

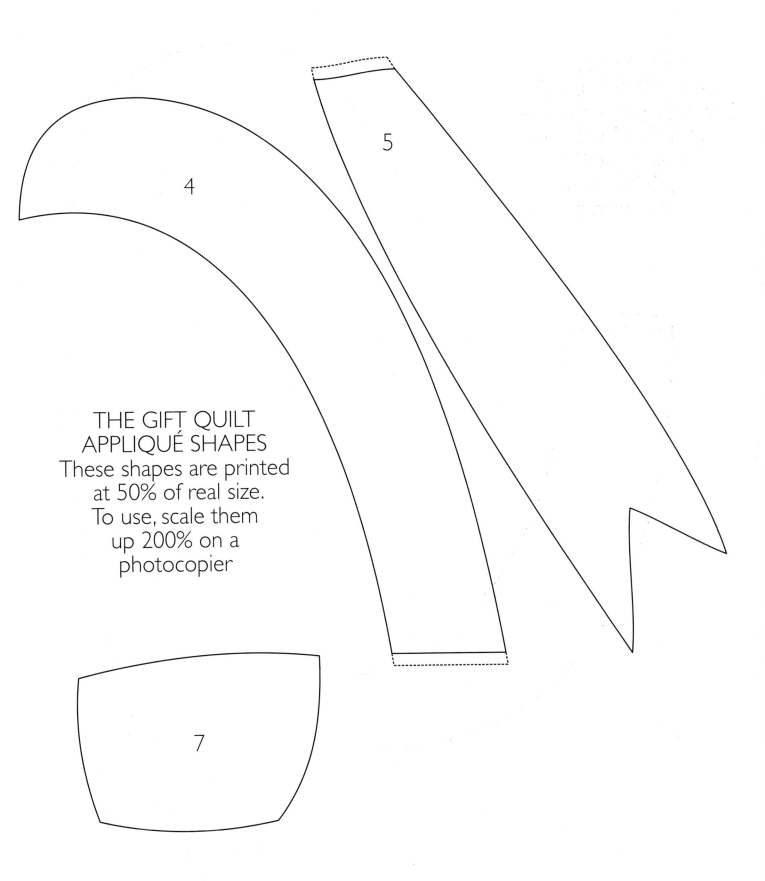

THE GIFT QUILT
APPLIQUÉ SHAPES
These shapes are printed
at 50% of real size.
To use, scale them
up 200% on a
photocopier

4

5

7

Patchwork Know How

These instructions are intended for the novice quilt maker, providing the basic information needed to make the projects in this book, along with some useful tips.

Preparing the fabric

Prewash all new fabrics before you begin, to ensure that there will be no uneven shrinkage and no bleeding of colours when the finished quilt is laundered. Press the fabric whilst it is still damp to return crispness to it. All fabric requirements in this book are calculated on a 40in (101.5cm) usable fabric width to allow for shrinkage and selvedge removal.

Making templates

Transparent template plastic is the best material, it is durable and allows you to see the fabric and select certain motifs. You can also use thin stiff cardboard.

Templates for machine piecing

1 Trace off the actual–sized template provided either directly on to template plastic, or tracing paper, and then on to thin cardboard. Use a ruler to help you trace off the straight cutting line, dotted seam line and grainlines. Some of the templates in this book were too large to print at full size, they have therefore been printed at half real size. Photocopy them at 200% before using.

2 Cut out the traced off template using a craft knife, ruler and a self–healing cutting mat.

3 Punch holes in the corners of the template, at each point on the seam line, using a hole punch.

Templates for hand piecing

• Make a template as for machine piecing, but do not trace off the cutting line. Use the dotted seam line as the outer edge of the template.

• This template allows you to draw the seam lines directly on to the fabric. The seam allowances can then be cut by eye around the patch.

Cutting the fabric

On the individual instructions for each patchwork, you will find a summary of all the patch shapes used.
Always mark and cut out any border and binding strips first, followed by the largest patch shapes and finally the smallest ones, to make the most efficient use of your fabric. The border and binding strips are best cut using a rotary cutter.

Rotary cutting

Rotary cut strips are usually cut across the fabric from selvedge to selvedge, but some projects may vary, so please read through all the instructions before you start cutting the fabrics.

1 Before beginning to cut, press out any folds or creases in the fabric. If you are cutting a large piece of fabric, you will need to fold it several times to fit the cutting mat. When there is only a single fold, place the fold facing you. If the fabric is too wide to be folded only once, fold it concertina–style until it fits your mat. A small rotary cutter with a sharp blade will cut up to 6 layers of fabric; a large cutter up to 8 layers.

2 To ensure that your cut strips are straight and even, the folds must be placed exactly parallel to the straight edges of the fabric and along a line on the cutting mat.

3 Place a plastic ruler over the raw edge of the fabric, overlapping it about ½in (1.25cm). Make sure that the ruler is at right angles to both the straight edges and the fold to ensure that you cut along the straight grain. Press down on the ruler and wheel the cutter away from yourself along the edge of the ruler.

4 Open out the fabric to check the edge. Don't worry if it's not perfectly straight, a little wiggle will not show when the quilt is stitched together. Re–fold fabric, then place the ruler over the trimmed edge, aligning edge with the markings on the ruler that match the correct strip width. Cut strip along the edge of the ruler.

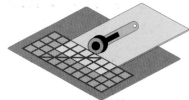

Using templates

The most efficient way to cut out templates is by first rotary cutting a strip of fabric the width stated for your template, and then marking off your templates along the strip, edge to edge at the required angle. This method leaves hardly any waste and gives a random effect to your patches. A less efficient method is to fussy cut, where the templates are cut individually by placing them on particular motifs or stripes, to create special effects. Although this method is more wasteful it yields very interesting results.

1 Place the template face down, on the wrong side of the fabric, with the grain line arrow following the straight grain of the fabric, if indicated. Be careful though – check with your individual instructions, as some instructions may ask you to cut patches on varying grains.

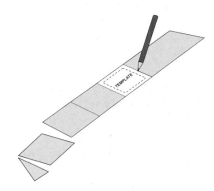

2 Hold the template firmly in place and draw around it with a sharp pencil or crayon, marking in the corner dots or seam lines. To save fabric, position patches close together or even touching. Don't worry if outlines positioned on the straight grain when drawn on striped fabrics do not always match the stripes when cut – this will add a degree of visual excitement to the patchwork!

3 Once you've drawn all the pieces needed, you are ready to cut the fabric, with either a rotary cutter and ruler, or a pair of sharp sewing scissors.

Basic hand and machine piecing

Patches can be joined together by hand or machine. Machine stitching is quicker, but hand assembly allows you to carry your patches around with you and work on them in every spare moment. The choice is yours. For techniques that are new to you, practise on scrap pieces of fabric until you feel confident

Machine piecing

Follow the quilt instructions for the order in which to piece the individual patchwork blocks and then assemble the blocks together in rows.

1 Seam lines are not marked on the fabric, so stitch ¼in (6mm) seams using the machine needle plate, a ¼in (6mm) wide machine foot, or tape stuck to the machine as a guide. Pin two patches with right sides together, matching edges.

Set your machine at 10–12 stitches per inch (2.5cm) and stitch seams from edge to edge, removing pins as you feed the fabric through **the machine.**

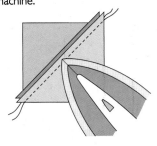

2 Press the seams of each patchwork block to one side before attempting to join it to another block.

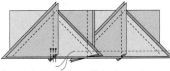

3 When joining rows of blocks, make sure that adjacent seam allowances are pressed in opposite directions to reduce bulk and make matching easier. Pin pieces together directly through the stitch line and to the right and left of the seam. Remove pins as you sew. Continue pressing seams to one side as you work.

Hand piecing

1 Pin two patches with right sides together, so that the marked seam lines are facing outwards.

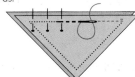

2 Using a single strand of strong thread, secure the corner of a seam line with a couple of back stitches.

3 Sew running stitches along the marked line, working 8–10 stitches per inch (2.5cm) and

ending at the opposite seam line corner with a few back stitches. When hand piecing never stitch over the seam allowances.

4 Press the seams to one side, as shown in machine piecing (Step 2).

Inset seams.

In some patchwork layouts a patch will have to be sewn into an angled corner formed by the joining of two other patches. Use the following method whether you are machine or hand piecing. Don't be intimidated – this is not hard to do once you have learned a couple of techniques. The seam is sewn from the centre outwards in two halves to ensure that no tucks appear at the centre.

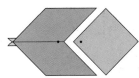

1 Mark with dots exactly where the inset will be joined and mark the seam lines on the wrong side of the fabric on the inset patch.

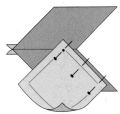

2 With right sides together and inset piece on top, pin through the dots to match the inset points. Pin the rest of the seam at right angles to the stitching line, along one edge of an adjoining patch.

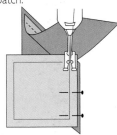

3 Stitch the patch in place along the seam line starting with the needle down through the inset point dots. Secure thread with a backstitch if hand piecing, or stitch forward for a few stitches before backstitching, when machine piecing.

4 Pivot the patch, to enable it to align with the adjacent side of the angled corner, allowing you work on the second half of the seam. Starting with a pin at the inset point once again. Pin and stitch the second side in place, as before. Check seams and press carefully.

Machine appliqué

Using adhesive web:

To make machine appliqué very easy you can use adhesive web, which comes attached to a paper backing sheet, to bond the motifs to the background fabric. This keeps the pieces in place whilst they are stitched.

1 Trace the reversed appliqué design onto the paper side of the adhesive web leaving a ¼in (6mm) gap between all the shapes. Roughly cut out the motifs ⅛in (3mm) outside your drawn line.

2 Bond the motifs to the reverse of your chosen fabrics. Cut out on the drawn line with very sharp scissors. Remove the backing paper by scoring in the centre of the motif carefully with a scissor point and peeling the paper away from the centre out, this prevents damage to the edges. Place the motifs onto the background noting any which may be layered. Cover with a clean cloth and bond with a hot iron (check instructions for temperature setting as adhesive web can vary depending on the manufacturer).

3 Using a contrasting or complimenting coloured thread in your machine, work small close zigzag stitches or a blanket stitch if your machine has one, around the edge of the motifs, the majority of the stitching should sit on the appliqué shape. When stitching up to points stop with the machine needle in the down position, lift the foot of your machine, pivot the work, lower the foot and continue to stitch. Make sure all the raw edges are stitched.

Hand appliqué

Good preparation is essential for speedy and accurate hand appliqué. The finger–pressing method is suitable for needle–turning application, used for simple shapes like leaves and flowers. Using a card template is the best method for bold simple motifs such as circles.

Finger-pressing:

1 To make your template, transfer the appliqué design on to stiff card using carbon paper, and cut out template. Trace around the outline of your appliquéd shape on to the right side of your fabric using a well sharpened pencil. Cut out shapes, adding a ¼in (6mm) seam allowance all around by eye.

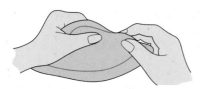

2 Hold shape right side up and fold under the seam, turning along your drawn line, pinch to form a crease. Dampening the fabric makes this very easy. When using shapes with 'points' such as leaves turn the seam allowance at the 'point' in first as shown in the diagram, then continue all round the shape. If your shapes have sharp curves you can snip the seam allowance to ease the curve. Take care not to stretch the appliqué shapes as you work.

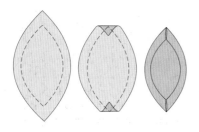

Card templates:

1 Cut out appliqué shapes as shown in step 1 of finger–pressing. Make a circular template from thin cardboard, without seam allowances.

2 Using a matching thread, work a row of running stitches close to the edge of the fabric circle. Place thin cardboard template in the centre of the fabric circle on the wrong side of the fabric.

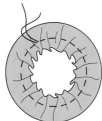

3 Carefully pull up the running stitches to gather up the edge of the fabric circle around the cardboard template. Press, so that no puckers or tucks appear on the right side. Then, carefully pop out the cardboard template without distorting the fabric shape.

Pressing stems:

For straight stems, place fabric face down and

simply press over the ¼in (6mm) seam allowance along each edge. You don't need to finish the ends of stems that are layered under other appliqué shapes. Where the end of the stem is visible simply tuck under the end and finish neatly.

Needle-turning application

1 Take the appliqué shape and pin in position. Stroke the seam allowance under with the tip of the needle as far as the creased pencil line, and hold securely in place with your thumb. Using a matching thread, bring the needle up from the back of the block into the edge of the shape and proceed to blind–hem in place. This is a stitch where the motifs appear to be held on invisibly. Bring the thread out from below through the folded edge of the motif, never on the top. The stitches must be worked small, even and close together to prevent the seam allowance from unfolding and frayed edges appearing. Try to avoid pulling the stitches too tight, as this will cause the motifs to pucker up. Work around the whole shape, stroking under each small section before sewing.

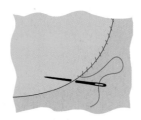

Quilting and finishing

When you have finished piecing your patchwork and added any borders, press it carefully. It is now ready for quilting.

Marking quilting designs and motifs

Many tools are available for marking quilting patterns, check the manufacturer's instructions for use and test on scraps of fabric from your project. Use an acrylic ruler for marking straight lines.

Stencils: Some designs require stencils, these can be made at home, by transferring the designs on to template plastic, or stiff cardboard. The design is then cut away in the form of long dashes, to act as guides for both internal and external lines. These stencils are a quick method for producing an identical set of repeated designs.

Preparing the backing and batting

• Remove the selvedges and piece together the backing fabric to form a backing at least 4in (10cm) larger all round than the patchwork top.

• For quilting choose a fairly thin batting, preferably pure cotton, to give your quilt a flat appearance. If your batting has been rolled up, unroll it and let it rest before cutting it to the same size as the backing.

• For a large quilt it may be necessary to join 2 pieces of batting to fit. Lay the pieces of batting on a flat surface so that they overlap by approx. 8in (20cm). Cut a curved line through both layers.

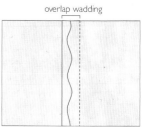

Carefully peel away the two narrow pieces and discard. Butt the curved cut edges back together. Stitch the two pieces together using a large herringbone stitch.

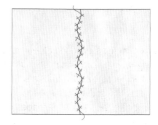

Basting the layers together

1 On a bare floor or large work surface, lay out the backing with wrong side uppermost. Use weights along the edges to keep it taut.

2 Lay the batting on the backing and smooth it out gently. Next lay the patchwork top, right side up, on top of the batting and smooth gently until there are no wrinkles. Pin at the corners and at the midpoints of each side, close to the edges.

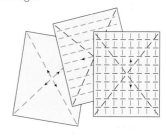

3 Beginning at the centre, baste diagonal lines outwards to the corners, making your stitches about 3in (7.5cm) long. Then, again starting at the centre, baste horizontal and vertical lines out to the edges. Continue basting until you have basted a grid of lines about 4in (10cm) apart over the entire quilt.

4 For speed, when machine quilting, some quilters prefer to baste their quilt sandwich layers together using rust–proof safety pins, spaced at 4in (10cm) intervals over the entire quilt.

Hand quilting

This is best done with the quilt mounted on a quilting frame or hoop, but as long as you have basted the quilt well, a frame is not essential. With the quilt top facing upwards, begin at the centre of the quilt and make even running stitches following the design. It is more important to make even stitches on both sides of the quilt than to make small ones. Start and finish your stitching with back stitches and bury the ends of your threads in the batting.

Machine quilting

• For a flat looking quilt, always use a walking foot on your machine for straight lines, and a darning foot for free–motion quilting.

• It's best to start your quilting at the centre of the quilt and work out towards the borders, doing the straight quilting lines first (stitch–in–the–ditch) followed by the free–motion quilting.

• When free motion quilting stitch in a loose meandering style as shown in the diagrams. Do not stitch too closely as this will make the quilt feel stiff when finished. If you wish you can include floral themes or follow shapes on the printed fabrics for added interest.

• Make it easier for yourself by handling the quilt properly. Roll up the excess quilt neatly to fit under your sewing machine arm, and use a table, or chair to help support the weight of the quilt that hangs down the other side.

Preparing to bind the edges

Once you have quilted or tied your quilt sandwich together, remove all the basting stitches. Then, baste around the outer edge of the quilt ¼in (6mm) from the edge of the top patchwork layer. Trim the back and batting to the edge of the patchwork and straighten the edge of the patchwork if necessary.

Making the binding

1 Cut bias or straight grain strips the width required for your binding, making sure the grainline is running the correct way on your straight grain strips. Cut enough strips until you have the required length to go around the edge of your quilt.

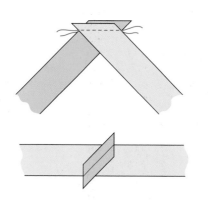

2 To join strips together, the two ends that are to be joined must be cut at a 45 degree angle, as above. Stitch right sides together, trim turnings and press seam open.

Binding the edges

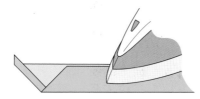

1 Cut the starting end of binding strip at a 45 degree angle, fold a ¼in (6mm) turning to wrong side along cut edge and press in place. With wrong sides together, fold strip in half lengthways, keeping raw edges level, and press.

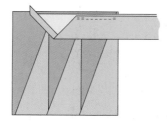

2 Starting at the centre of one of the long edges, place the doubled binding on to the right side of the quilt keeping raw edges level. Stitch the binding in place starting ¼in (6mm) in from the diagonal folded edge (see above). Reverse stitch to secure, and working ¼in (6mm) in from edge of the quilt towards first corner of quilt. Stop ¼in (6mm) in from corner and work a few reverse stitches.

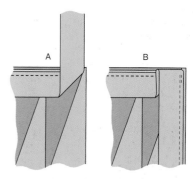

3 Fold the loose end of the binding up, making a 45 degree angle (see A). Keeping the diagonal fold in place, fold the binding back down, aligning the raw edges with the next side of the quilt. Starting at the point where the last stitch ended, stitch down the next side (see B).

4 Continue to stitch the binding in place around all the quilt edges in this way, tucking the finishing end

of the binding inside the diagonal starting section (see above).

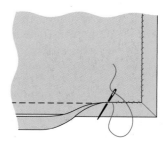

5 Turn the folded edge of the binding on to the back of the quilt. Hand stitch the folded edge in place just covering binding machine stitches, and folding a mitre at each corner.

Glossary of Terms

Appliqué The technique of stitching fabric shapes on to a background to create a design. It can be applied either by hand or machine with a decorative embroidery stitch, such as buttonhole, or satin stitch.

Backing The bottom layer of a quilt sandwich. It is made of fabric pieced to the size of the quilt top with the addition of about 3in (7.5cm) all around to allow for quilting take–up.

Basting or Tacking This is a means of holding two fabric layers or the layers of a quilt sandwich together temporarily with large hand stitches, or pins.

Batting or Wadding This is the middle layer, or padding in a quilt. It can be made of cotton, wool, silk or synthetic fibres.

Bias The diagonal grain of a fabric. This is the direction which has the most give or stretch, making it ideal for bindings, especially on curved edges.

Binding A narrow strip of fabric used to finish off the edges of quilts or projects; it can be cut on the straight grain of a fabric or on the bias.

Block A single design unit that when stitched together with other blocks create the quilt top. It is most often a square, hexagon, or rectangle, but it can be any shape. It can be pieced or plain.

Border A frame of fabric stitched to the outer edges of the quilt top. Borders can be narrow or wide, pieced or plain. As well as making the quilt larger, they unify the overall design and draw attention to the central area.

Chalk pencils Available in various colours, they are used for marking lines, or spots on fabric.

Cutting mat Designed for use with a rotary cutter, it is made from a special 'self–healing' material that keeps your cutting blade sharp. Cutting mats come in various sizes and are usually marked with a grid to help you line up the edges of fabric and cut out larger pieces.

Design Wall Used for laying out fabric patches before sewing. A large wall or folding board covered with flannel fabric or cotton batting in a neutral shade (dull beige or grey work well) will hold fabric in place so that an overall view can be taken of the placement.

Free–motion quilting Curved wavy quilting lines stitched in a random manner. Stitching diagrams are often given for you to follow as a loose guide.

Fussy cutting This is when a template is placed on a particular motif, or stripe, to obtain interesting effects. This method is not as efficient as strip cutting, but yields very interesting results.

Grain The direction in which the threads run in a woven fabric. In a vertical direction it is called the lengthwise grain, which has very little stretch. The horizontal direction, or crosswise grain is slightly stretchy, but diagonally the fabric has a lot of stretch. This grain is called the bias. Wherever possible the grain of a fabric should run in the same direction on a quilt block and borders.

Inset seams or setting–in A patchwork technique whereby one patch (or block) is stitched into a 'V' shape formed by the joining of two other patches (or blocks).

Patch A small shaped piece of fabric used in the making of a patchwork pattern.

Patchwork The technique of stitching small pieces of fabric (patches) together to create a larger piece of fabric, usually forming a design.

Pieced quilt A quilt composed of patches.

Quilting Traditionally done by hand with running stitches, but for speed modern quilts are often stitched by machine. The stitches are sewn through the top, wadding and backing to hold the three layers together. Quilting stitches are usually worked in some form of design, but they can be random.

Quilting hoop Consists of two wooden circular or oval rings with a screw adjuster on the outer ring. It stabilises the quilt layers, helping to create an even tension.

Rotary cutter A sharp circular blade attached to a handle for quick, accurate cutting. It is a device that can be used to cut up to six layers of fabric at one time. It must be used in conjunction with a 'self–healing' cutting mat and a thick plastic ruler.

Rotary ruler A thick, clear plastic ruler printed with lines that are exactly $\frac{1}{4}$in (6mm) apart. Sometimes they also have diagonal lines printed on, indicating 45 and 60 degree angles. A rotary ruler is used as a guide when cutting out fabric pieces using a rotary cutter.

Sashing A piece or pieced sections of fabric interspaced between blocks.

Sashing Posts When blocks have sashing between them the corner squares are known as sashing posts.

Selvedges Also known as selvages, these are the firmly woven edges down each side of a fabric length. Selvedges should be trimmed off before cutting out your fabric, as they are more liable to shrink when the fabric is washed.

Stitch–in–the–ditch or Ditch quilting Also known as quilting–in–the–ditch. The quilting stitches are worked along the actual seam lines, to give a pieced quilt texture.

Template A pattern piece used as a guide for marking and cutting out fabric patches, or marking a quilting, or appliqué design. Usually made from plastic or strong card that can be reused many times.

Threads One hundred percent cotton or cotton–covered polyester is best for hand and machine piecing. Choose a colour that matches your fabric. When sewing different colours and patterns together, choose a medium to light neutral colour, such as grey or ecru. Specialist quilting threads are available for hand and machine quilting.

Walking foot or Quilting foot This is a sewing machine foot with dual feed control. It is very helpful when quilting, as the fabric layers are fed evenly from the top and below, reducing the risk of slippage and puckering.

Biographies

Betsy Rickles

Betsy began quilting in the late 90's. She found that piecing the quilt became the foundation of the project and that the free motion quilting, inspired by the movement in Kaffe's fabrics, made the design come alive. She likes using the solid shot cottons from Kaffe's collections as backing, not only do the quilting designs really pop but it's like quilting through butter. Betsy lives near Sisters, Oregon, and has worked for Jean and Valori Wells of the Stitchin' Post.

Pauline Smith

Pauline Smith has been a quilt maker and designer since a college visit to The American Museum in Bath in 1968. She makes most of Kaffe's quilts for the Rowan Patchwork And Quilting books, and as the Rowan patchwork co-ordinator, she works closely with everyone involved in producing the 'Patchwork and Quilting' series.

Sally Davis

Sally began quiltmaking in 1980 after experimenting with every known craft. It quickly became a love affair and passion. Sally owned a quilt shop called Quilt Connection where she met Liza and Kaffe and over 9 years encompassed her love of colour with their style and fabrics. Two of her quilts were featured in Rowan P&Q 4 and a Colourful Journey. After closing the store 2 years ago, Sally has been travelling around the country teaching and lecturing as well as working with Liza.

Roberta Horton

Roberta Horton of Berkeley, California has been a quiltmaker for over 30 years. She has taught and lectured worldwide. Her study and love of quilts has pushed her into developing many workshops and to the authoring of six books. Roberta was the recipient of the 2000 Silver Star Award presented by the International Quilt Association. This was in recognition of her lifetime body of work and the long-term effect it has had on quilting.

Brandon Mably

A regular contributor to the Rowan Patchwork books Brandon Mably has built a reputation as a quilt designer of simple, elegant quilts in restful colours. Brandon trained at The Kaffe Fassett Studio. He designs for the Rowan and Vogue Knitting magazine knitwear collections, and is the author of *Brilliant Knits* and *Knitting Color*.

Mary Mashuta

California quiltmaker Mary Mashuta has been making quilts and wearables for over thirty years. She is a professionally trained teacher who has been teaching internationally since 1985. Her classes always stress easily understood colour and design. She knows that no quilter can own too much fabric, and she enjoys discovering new blocks to showcase personal collections. Mary has authored five books and numerous magazine articles.

Jane Brocket

Jane Brocket is an enthusiastic amateur quilt maker. Five year ago, inspired by Kaffe Fassett and Liza Prior Lucy, she started making simple, colourful quilts which are much used and enjoyed by her family. She is mostly self-taught and prefers to use lovely fabrics and simple patterns. She has written about her quilting thoughts and processes, and the results (as well as her other creative endeavours such as knitting, crochet, embroidery, baking and gardening) in her book *The Gentle Art of Domesticity* (Hodder & Stoughton, 2007).

Liza Prior Lucy

Liza Prior Lucy first began making quilts in 1990. She was so enthralled by the craftspeople she met and by the generously stocked quilt fabric shops in the States that quiltmaking soon became a passion. Liza originally trained as a knitwear designer and produced features for needlework magazines. She also owned and operated her own needlepoint shop in Washington, D.C.
Liza met Kaffe when she was working as a sales representative for Rowan Yarns. They worked closely together to write and produce the quilts for the books *Glorious Patchwork*, *Passionate Patchwork* and *Kaffe Fassett's V&A Quilts*.

Experience Ratings

★ Easy, straightforward, suitable for a beginner.

★ ★ Suitable for the average patchworker and quilter.

★ ★ ★ For the more experienced patchworker and quilter.

Acknowledgements

We give a special thanks to Perry Rodriguez and all the staff and gardeners at Great Dixter for making us so welcome when photographing this book and also for giving us free rein to place the quilts anywhere we wanted (even in the flowerbeds!).

Great Dixter House and Gardens is run by a Charitable Trust and is open to the public. For details of opening times, events and for information about supporting Great Dixter by becoming a friend, check out their website, www.greatdixter.co.uk.

All Drima and Sylko machine threads, Anchor embroidery threads, and Prym sewing aids, distributed in UK by Coats Crafts UK, P.O. Box 22, Lingfield House, Lingfield Point, McMullen Road, Darlington, Co. Durham, DL1 1YQ.
Consumer helpline: 01325 394237.

Anchor embroidery thread and Coats sewing threads, distributed in the USA by Coats & Clark,
3430 Toringdon Way, Charlotte, North Carolina 28277.
Tel: 704 329 5800.
Fax: 704 329 5027.

Prym products distributed in the USA by Prym-Dritz Corp,
950 Brisack Road, Spartanburg, SC 29303.
Tel: +1 864 576 5050. Fax: +1 864 587 3353,
e-mail: pdmar@teleplex.net

R O W A N

Green Lane Mill, Holmfirth, West Yorkshire, England
Tel: +44 (0) 1484 681881   Fax: +44 (0) 1484 687920   Internet: www.knitrowan.com
Email: mail@knitrowan.com

Printed Fabrics

When ordering printed fabrics please note the following codes which precede the fabric number and two digit colour code.

GP is the code for the Kaffe Fassett collection

PJ is the code for the Philip Jacobs collection

The fabric collection can be viewed online at the following

www.westminsterfibers.com

QUILT INSTRUCTION CODES		AMERICAN CODES
Woven Haze Stripe		
Persimmon	HZS01	S4481
Mustard	HZS02	S4503
Sunshine	HZS06	S4519
Raspberry	HZS12	S4482
Green	HZS16	S4516
Lavender	HZS17	S4475
Pine	HZS19	S4490
Aegean	HZS20	S4491
Woven Tone Stripe		
Citrus	WTSCN	W2TONE.CITRUS
Gold	WTSGD	W2TONE.GOLD
Magenta	WTSMG	W2TONE. MAGEN
Moss	WTSMS	W2TONE.MOSS
Ochre	WTSOC	W2TONE.OCHRE
Pumpkin	WTSPN	W2TONE.PUMPK
Purple	WTSPU	W2TONE.PURPLE
Red	WTSRD	W2TONE.REDD
Spice	WTSSI	W2TONE.SPICE
Suede	WTSSD	W2TONE.SUEDE
Printed Ikat		
Red	PKDRD	ICKBDI.REDD

Distributors and Stockists

Overseas Distributors of Rowan Fabrics

ARGENTINA
Coats Crafts Brazil
Rua do Manifesto,
705 Ipiranga
Sao Paulo
SP 04209-000

AUSTRALIA
XLN Fabrics
2/21 Binney Road,
Kings Park
New South Wales 2148
Tel: 61 2 96213066
Email: info@xln.co.zu

AUSTRIA
Rhinetex
Geurdeland 7
6673 DR Andelst
The Netherlands
Tel: 31 488 480030
Email: info@rhinetex.com

BELGIUM
Rhinetex
Geurdeland 7
6673 DR Andelst
The Netherlands
Tel: 31 488 480030
Email: info@rhinetex.com

BRAZIL
Coats Crafts Brazil
Rua do Manifesto,
705 Ipiranga
Sao Paulo
SP 04209-000

CANADA
Telio
625 Rue DesLauriers
Montreal, QC, Canada
Tel: 514 271 4607
Email: info@telio.com

CHILE
Coats Crafts Brazil
Rua do Manifesto,
705 Ipiranga
Sao Paulo
SP 04209-000

COLUMBIA
Coats Crafts Brazil
Rua do Manifesto,
705 Ipiranga
Sao Paulo
SP 04209-000

DENMARK
Coats HP A/S
Nannasgade 28
2200 Copenhagen N

FRANCE
Rhinetex
Geurdeland 7
6673 DR Andelst
The Netherlands
Tel: 31 488 480030
Email: info@rhinetex.com

GERMANY
Rhinetex
Geurdeland 7
6673 DR Andelst
The Netherlands
Tel: 31 488 480030
Email: info@rhinetex.com

HOLLAND
Rhinetex
Geurdeland 7
6673 DR Andelst
The Netherlands
Tel: 31 488 480030
Email: info@rhinetex.com

ICELAND
Storkurinn
Laugavegi 59
101 Reykjavik
Tel: 354 551 8258

ITALY
Coats Italy
Via Vespucci 2
20124 Milano
MILANO
Tel: 02 636 15224

JAPAN
Kiyohara & Co Ltd
4-5-5 Minamikyuhoji-Machi
Chuo-Ku
OSAKA
541-8506
Tel: 81 6 6251 7179

LUXEMBOURG
Rhinetex
Geurdeland 7
6673 DR Andelst
The Netherlands
Tel: 31 488 480030
Email: info@rhinetex.com

NEW ZEALAND
Fabco Limited
280 School Road
Waimauku
AUCKLAND 1250
Tel: 64 9 411 9996
Email: info@fabco.co.nz

NORWAY
Coats Knappehuset AS
Pb 100 Ulset
5873 Bergen
Tel: 00 47 555 393 00

POLAND
Coats Polska Sp.z.o.o
ul. Kaczencowa 16
91-214 Lodz
Tel: 48 42 254 03 0400

PORTUGAL
Companhia de Linhas Coats & Clark
Quinta de Cravel
4430-968 Villa Nova de Gaia
Tel: 0351 223770700

SINGAPORE
Quilts and Calicoes
163 Tanglin Road
03-13 Tanglin Mall
247933
Tel: 65 68874708

SOUTH KOREA
Coats Korea Co Ltd,
5F Kuckdong B/D,
935-40 Bangbae-Dong,
Seocho-Gu, Seoul.
Tel: 82 2 521 6262

SOUTH AFRICA
Arthur Bales PTY Ltd
62 4th Avenue
PO Box 44644
Linden 2104
Tel: 27 11 888 2401

SPAIN
Coats Fabra
Sant Adria, 20
E-08030 Barcelona
Tel: 00 34 93 290 84 00

SWITZERLAND
Rhinetex
Geurdeland 7
6673 DR Andelst
The Netherlands
Tel: 31 488 480030
Email: info@rhinetex.com

SWEDEN
Coats Expotex AB
Stationsv gen 2
516 31 Dalsj fors
Tel: 46 337 207 900

TAIWAN
Long Teh Trading Co
No. 71 Hebei W. St
Beitun District
Taichung City
Tel: 886 4 2247 7711

UK
Rowan
Green Lane Mill
Holmfirth
HD9 2DX
United Kingdom
Tel: +44(0) 1484 681881
Internet: www.knitrowan.com
Email: mail@knitrowan.com

U.S.A
Westminster Fibers
3430 Toringdon Way
Suite 301,
Charlotte,
NC 28277
Tel: 704-329-5822
Email: fabric@westminsterfibers.com
Internet: westminsterfibers.com